FUNDAMENTALS

A GUIDE FOR PARENTS, TEACHERS AND CARERS ON MENTAL HEALTH AND SELF-ESTEEM

NATASHA DEVON AND LYNN CRILLY

JOHN BLAKE

Published by John Blake Publishing Ltd,
3 Bramber Court, 2 Bramber Road,
London W14 9PB, England

www.johnblakepublishing.co.uk

www.facebook.com/johnblakebooks 🅵
twitter.com/jblakebooks 🆃

This edition published in 2015

ISBN: 978 1 78418 118 5

British Library Cataloguing-in-Publication Data:

A catalogue record for this book is available from the British Library.

Design by www.envydesign.co.uk

Printed in Great Britain by CPI Group (UK) Ltd

1 3 5 7 9 10 8 6 4 2

Papers used by John Blake Publishing are natural, recyclable products made
from wood grown in sustainable forests. The manufacturing processes
conform to the environmental regulations of the country of origin.

Every attempt has been made to contact the relevant
copyright-holders, but some were unobtainable. We would be grateful
if the appropriate people could contact us.

ABOUT THE AUTHORS

 Natasha Devon is a journalist, TV pundit, and founder of The Self-Esteem Team, who have taught self-esteem classes to more than 40,000 teenagers in schools, colleges and universities throughout the UK, as well as their parents and teachers. She works alongside the All Parties Parliamentary Group on Body Image and campaigns for good body image and mental health practice in education and in the media. The Self-Esteem Team were given an award at the House of Commons in 2014 in recognition of their services to education. Natasha has been named a Mental Health Association 'Hero', one of Ernst & Young's Top 50 Social Entrepreneurs and *Cosmopolitan* magazine's Ultimate Woman of the Year.

She lives in West London with her partner Marcus and several David Bowie posters.

Lynn Crilly lives in Surrey with her husband Kevin and their twin daughters, Charlotte and Samantha. Through using her unique and very effective form of counselling she has established herself as one of the country's leading private therapists, working with people from all walks of life, ages and genders. She is admired for her passion and understanding – something she attributes to the strength and loyalty of her family and friends, with whom she spends as much time as possible.

Lynn is a trustee for the charity Men Get Eating Disorders Too, has received a B-eat Award, and been named 'Inspirational Mother of the Year'.

'What really shines through is the love of a mother, over and above being an author, therapist and business woman. Lynn is a loving mum, and that alone I think trumps all the clever science in the world… Read it. Heed it.'

Dedicated to Jess, my star student.
Your creativity, kindness and individuality continue
to inspire me long after my lesson inspired you
to conquer your demons.
– Natasha

CONTENTS

INTRODUCTION

On a chilly November evening about five years ago, I was walking along the main road which led from Liverpool Street station to my then-home in East London. A man with a friendly face walking in the opposite direction said 'Excuse me?' and despite the cold, darkness and everything my mother has told me about not talking to strangers, something made me stop and say 'Yes?'.

'I just wanted to tell you that you look lovely,' he said. I thanked him, he turned on his heel and walked away. The entire exchange must have delayed me by about ten seconds.

As I continued marching home, suddenly a firework shot out of a side street, directly across my path. If I had been on my original trajectory and not had that brief conversation with the stranger, the firework would have hit me.

I've come to see that experience as a metaphor for my job. If

I can convince young people just to pause briefly in the darkness to consider what I tell them, then perhaps I might prevent them from being damaged by some of the things that life will throw at them (whilst also giving them the message that they look lovely).

If my role is that of the stranger who delivers a positive message on life's journey, then parents, carers and teachers are the constant companions guiding young people along the path.

In our complex and often toxic culture, there's so much pressure for the adults who are guiding young people to be 'perfect'. There are a gazillion conflicting messages being fired at you from all angles and most are placing every conceivable blame squarely at your door. The world will find infinite ways to tell you that you aren't good enough, if you give it even an iota of a chance.

The truth is no one gets it right a hundred per cent of the time. No matter how comprehensively you try and cater to your young charge's needs, there will be some things that you cannot control, some lessons they need to learn on their own and they'll inevitably emerge from their coming-of-age a tiny bit fucked-up (because being a tiny bit fucked-up is actually a crucial part of being a human being).

This book is all about the things you **can** do. Most of the changes we'd encourage you to make are simple and easy to implement, yet they'll dramatically transform the culture of your home, your school and most importantly, your mind. By tweaking the language that we use and examining the way we understand and communicate about self-esteem and mental illness, we can help build the armour young people need to navigate their lives happily and healthily.

According to a study, in an average British classroom in

2011 three students were self-harming. Eating disorders will be experienced by one in ten young people before they reach the age of twenty-five. Suicide is the biggest killer of men and boys under twenty-one in the UK. Ten percent of the British population currently meet the diagnostic criteria for mixed depression and anxiety disorder.

I could go on but I won't because, ironically, to do so would be too depressing. For whilst my work delivering self-esteem classes to teenagers over the past eight years has, sadly, completely borne out the above statistics, it has also taught me to hope. Our young people are brilliant. If you're a parent reading this, thanks so much for making them – they are a pleasure to interact with every day.

Children and teenagers have an ability to adapt and the flexibility to allow themselves to think in unfamiliar ways, making them the proverbial leopards who CAN in fact change their spots. They have an optimism and enthusiasm for life which you can really only have when you have not yet experienced a grey pubic hair or had to pay your own Council Tax. They have been more sensitive, more emotionally intelligent and more insightful than I could ever have anticipated.

In my experience, all most young folk need is a little guidance, a bit of clarity, reassurance that they're valued, a safe environment to express how they feel and a couple of really good role models. This book aims to give you the information and tools you need to provide those things.

Natasha Devon

ABOUT YOUR AUTHORS

This book is somewhat unusual, in that it is a collaboration between two authors, Natasha Devon and Lynn Crilly. We'll make sure there is an indicator above each section so you know who is speaking when. We should be easy to distinguish, just look for the swearing (that's Natasha) and *Lynn's sections appear in italics like this.*

As a very broad guide, Lynn's advice is aimed mostly at parents and carers, focusing on the home environment and Natasha's at teachers and on educational environments. There's a lot of cross-over, though, so we'd suggest you read everything. It seems a shame not to, after you've bought the book and everything.

We hope that, between the two of us, we have a comprehensive understanding of our subject matter. Here is a little about each of us:

Lynn

Ten years ago, I was a housewife and ran the office side of our family scaffolding business. I was constantly trying to find a work/life balance, but no more than any other working Mum. Approaching forty, I had a wonderful happy life with my husband Kevin and our beautiful twin daughters Charlotte and Samantha. Of course, like everyone, life threw challenges our way, but we always worked together to overcome them and move forward.

From the outside looking in, people used to think we had a 'perfect' existence. So, when in 2004 our Samantha was diagnosed with the early stages of anorexia nervosa our world fell apart. I had no idea how to deal with eating disorders back then, but my husband and I believed if we entrusted Sam's health to the 'system' she would get better – we had no reason to think otherwise at this point.

We tried everything to help Sam, taking her to our local GP (who was wonderfully supportive) and to both private and NHS clinics, but sadly nothing was working. I felt completely helpless watching our beautiful daughter become a shadow of her former self.

At the end of my tether and with my family falling apart I decided that there was no substitute for a mother's intuition and love. I took the decision to rehabilitate Sam myself with the support of our GP, friends and family. It was the steepest learning curve I could ever have anticipated. Looking back, it was quite a controversial thing to do, I suppose, but at the time my instinct told me it was the right way to get my little girl better.

I worked closely with Sam's school, knowing it was important to keep her in as normal an environment as possible. Everyone involved worked as a team throughout the recovery process. Step by step, Samantha slowly came back to us and began to leave behind the illness that had had such a profound effect, not only on her but on all of us.

As Sam went into recovery, it occurred to me that there wasn't much support for the carers, friends and family of those who suffer from eating disorders. It seemed to me that we were all feeling around in the dark, not knowing what we were supposed to say or do. Every website, book, or support group I could find focused only on the person experiencing the illness. I was also deeply troubled by the fact that Charlotte, my husband, and I were at times all made to feel that Sam's illness had been our fault. There is so much blame flung around and those closest to the sufferer are often an easy target.

So, I went on to do some studying of my own, including training as a Master of NLP (Neuro-linguistic Programming – a type of therapy). I was keen to work with other sufferers and their families, giving them the unconditional support and complete lack of judgement that my own experience had taught me was necessary. I also wrote and published my first book Hope with Eating Disorders *which is a self-help guide for parents and carers and it has gone on to sell all around the globe.*

Since then, I have set up a counselling practice and opened my doors to anyone struggling to deal with any type of mental illness, whether it's them experiencing the illness, or a loved one.

Looking back, although Sam had left her anorexia behind, she never truly felt comfortable in her skin until recently, when she reignited her love for drama and the arts. We have watched her grow into a beautiful, confident and vibrant young lady, pursuing a passion that allows her to express herself. As a parent, I am hugely relieved – being happy and healthy is all I have ever wanted for my children. I have also come to understand how helpful both sport and the arts can be in overcoming mental health issues.

Although my family at times have been pushed to the limit, we have always managed to emerge stronger for it. I have learned the importance of constant communication and that in fact there is no such thing as the 'perfect' family. Trying to be perfect is not only unrealistic, it can be dangerous.

Kevin my husband has never really understood mental illness (and never pretended to) but has still been able to provide unconditional support, without which we could never have survived. Charlotte has also been key to Sam's recovery and now works alongside me to develop more understanding for what a sufferer's family go through, with the empathy that can only come from first-hand experience.

When I spoke out about what we had experienced within our family, I learned that most people I knew were struggling with something behind closed doors. They had been too afraid to talk about it for fear of judgement. It was then that I realised how widespread problems like self-harm, anxiety, depression, OCD and eating disorders are and how confusing the wealth of information available on these subjects can be.

Over the past few years I have had the privilege of working with some wonderful people and their families, each and every one of them unique. Whilst I have been able to support them through their journeys, I too have learned from them. My clients and friends have said that they find my practical and down-to-earth approach really refreshing. I have been compared to the therapist in the film The King's Speech *many a time! His methods are unorthodox – but they get results.*

So here I am, ten years later and (at the time of writing this) nearly fifty – if you had told me ten years ago that I would be doing what I am doing today I would not have believed you. I do not pretend to be an expert on everything and I am still learning, but I hope with the benefit of my experience, knowledge and training I can help the people around me and you, the reader, work towards a happier and healthier future.

Natasha

As a seventeen-year-old sixth former I was confident, happy, healthy and looking forward to university (with ambitions to be Prime Minister and grades to match). Aged twenty-five I was a part-time model (of extremely limited success) with depression, bulimia, no money, no friends and no prospects. I'm not someone who likes to dwell on the particulars of the intervening years – I don't find the traditional tabloid-style approach of trying to shock the reader with weights, measurements and generalised disgustingness particularly informative or helpful. In fact, in a lot of cases it perversely gives people in the grips of eating disorders something to aim for.

The only really relevant moral to be taken away from my story is this – it was a gigantic waste of my life and my potential. I was as far away from the prevailing stereotype of someone who suffers from a mental illness as you can possibly imagine. Yet being completely unprepared for the world and its challenges robbed me of what should have been the best years of my life.

Instead of spending my late teens and early twenties doing the things you're supposed to do – studying, travelling, befriending, laughing, shagging and generally expanding the mind – I had my head wedged in various toilets throughout the British Isles.

It took almost eight years for me to find the necessary steely resolve to get better. I had three months of intensive therapy (a combination of NLP, CBT (Cognitive Behavioural Therapy) and hypnosis). After that, I spent about a year rediscovering who I was. My illness had become my identity and so without it I felt like the embodiment of a blank canvas.

I experimented with food and exercise to eventually find a balance in the glorious Middle Ground which can be so elusive in our 'I'll start the diet on Monday' culture. I went shopping, dyed my hair about seventeen different colours (sometimes all at once), moved to London with £100 in my bank account (which horrified my parents at the time) and generally stomped around in my Kurt Geiger ankle boots looking for inspiration. At the end of that process, I had established a relationship between my head and body and I knew without question that I wanted to be three things: A writer, someone who makes a tangible difference to the life of young people and a size 16.

I began studying psychology. I went back to my former (all girls') school, the Hertfordshire & Essex High School in Bishop's Stortford, and spent two weeks chatting to the students there, asking them what they felt was missing from their PSHE (Personal, Health and Social Education) and how they would like to be taught it.

The answers were fairly unanimous – they were tired of 'awareness-raising' lessons and television programmes on issues like self-harm and anorexia, which seemed to endlessly present problems with no practical solutions. What they wanted instead was something more universally relevant on body image, as well as pragmatic advice on how to feel more confident. I then went to a local all-boys' school (The Bishop's Stortford High School, fact fans) and repeated exactly the same process with the students there.

You must bear in mind that this was before I'd ever heard the world's most fabulous humanitarian Gok Wan utter the phrase 'boooodycooooonfidence' with that sassy little inflection of his, so I feared that when I took my lesson mainstream the World of Education would simply look at me blankly before shooing me away, telling me they had important things to teach, like algebra and stuff. Fortunately, that couldn't have been further from what happened. Teachers (literally, in some instances) leaped on me, telling me over and over again how this was 'so needed' in their school.

Today, I go into three schools or colleges per week on average and, owing to beyond-anticipated-even-by-me popular demand, have trained two other team members, Nadia and Grace, to deliver the sessions. We call ourselves the Self-Esteem Team (although Grace wanted it to be 'The Self E-Steam Train'. The only other person I know who gets this is the author Dominic Utton, who wrote an entire – extremely good and funny – book about trains). At the request of the places we've worked, we now also offer sessions for teachers and parents and we're constantly evolving and adapting according to the feedback we receive, the latest research and seismic cultural shifts (like the invention of Kim Kardashian's bum).

I've been into the independent institutions which immediately make one think 'Hogwarts!' and contain the sons and daughters of minor royalty, the inner-city schools situated in the centres of council estates where pupils' bags have to be checked for weaponry at the entrance, and every conceivable British educational facility in-between. Whilst the environments, the facilities and the staff are wildly different, the teenagers are invariably the same. Of course one has to edit the lesson, making the themes relevant and engaging to audiences of different ages and backgrounds but, as a general rule, self-esteem issues know no class, gender or sexuality. They're equal opportunity obstacles.

When I'm not teaching, I write freelance for newspapers (a few of my relevant articles are included in this book) and do some television punditry. At the time of writing, I also have a monthly column in *Cosmopolitan* magazine. It's called 'The Last Word' and has been described (by me) as '*a gloriously unbridled five hundred word rant on the last page of the magazine*'. It makes me more happy than you can imagine that my writing now appears in what is undoubtedly the publication equivalent of my Spiritual Home, *Cosmo* representing for me a place where one can care about social issues and be unapologetically fabulous simultaneously.

Today, I work alongside the All Parties Parliamentary Group on Body Image. I'm endlessly haranguing the government to give more priority and funding to health and social care in schools and I'm not opposed to using the force of my media profile to do it. I know from first-hand experience that, without the right guidance, even the brightest young person cannot fulfil their academic or personal potential. I consider myself very lucky that I was able to bring myself back from the abyss. Others, I know, are not so fortunate.

I will not stop until every teenager can enjoy the benefit of an equal and excellent PSHE programme.

Or until I die.

Or until Michael Gove says '*yeah.....sorry about that*'.

Whichever comes first.

CHAPTER 1

WHAT IS SELF-ESTEEM?

'Self-esteem isn't being cocky, just a lot happier and smiling and laughing more than someone who has low self-esteem.' *Florence, 13*

Lynn

If I had to define self-esteem in one sentence, I'd say it is how we perceive our value to the world and to others. We all have an idea of how much we are worth, both within the scope of our personal relationships, but also more widely as part of society.

Low self-esteem can be a debilitating condition that stops an individual from realising their full potential in all aspects of their life. A person with low self-esteem feels unworthy, incapable or incompetent, usually all three. In fact, a person with low self-esteem can feel so low about themselves this can actually perpetuate those feelings and the whole thing becomes a vicious circle.

Physically, low self-esteem can show itself in the way people hold themselves. They can sometimes be hunched over or trying to blend into the background. It's a common misconception that people with low self-esteem are always quiet and shy, though. Sometimes the loudest person in the room is trying to hide their feelings of low self-worth with a mask of apparent super-confidence that they present to the world.

As a general rule, someone with low self-esteem will avoid eye contact. There's an old saying that people who can't look you in the eye have something to hide. This is broadly true, but not for the reasons you might think. People with low self-esteem believe that they are unlovable, they have often convinced themselves that there is something fundamentally 'ugly' or shameful about them that, if you look them directly in the eye, you will be able to see. They quite often think everyone around them is cleverer or more competent than they are and that they are constantly trying to cover up their understanding of themselves as a 'fraud'. If you have a friend with low self-esteem, you're likely to feel frustrated that you rarely get to see 'the real them', because they aren't confident enough to allow their true selves to be seen.

A negative view of life is a key signifier of low self-esteem. If one does not feel positive about oneself it's very difficult to take a positive view of the world one inhabits. As well as complaining about life generally, quite often those with low self-esteem describe themselves using hyper-critical terms. They will say things like 'I'm stupid' or 'I'm ugly' as a matter of course, often quite flippantly. They'll also instantly dismiss and reject any compliments they receive. As a result of this, there is a tendency to compare themselves to their peers in an unfavourable way. They'll quite often claim they 'can't' do something before they have even tried or that that they 'don't want to' because they secretly fear they will make a fool of themselves. A fear of trying new things and taking risks quite often emerges out of this attitude, as is being unable to accept even the smallest of failures.

For the above reasons, it's often hard for those with low self-esteem to adapt to change. Having said that, they'll also probably have difficulty seeing challenges through. So whilst on the one hand they'll be reticent to changes, on the other they might seem to be 'chopping and changing' their minds constantly. Both making a decision and sticking to it are often difficult.

'For me, self-esteem is knowing you are in control of your destiny and feeling proud to be shaping my own.'
Annabel, 18

A person with low self-esteem will often have difficulties making decisions because they don't trust their own judgement. They will prefer to let others around them take the lead. This plays into the fear of failure, too – if other people take away the responsibility for our decision-making we can never be blamed for what happens as a consequence.

If someone suffers low self-esteem they might find it hard to keep friendships, although not necessarily hard to make them in the first place. I've seen those with self-esteem and mental illnesses gravitate towards one another, forming intense, short-lived connections which tend to burn out very quickly. The 'perfectionism' that is often talked about in relation to low self-esteem shows itself in the way personal relationships are formed, too. Those in the grips of low self-esteem tend to go one of two ways; they will either have very little tolerance for what they perceive to be weakness in others, or conversely they will tolerate other people's bullying or bad behaviour to the point where they become a victim. They can have an 'all or nothing' approach and for that reason are often found striving for a goal that is completely unrealistic. Similarly, they have unrealistic expectations of the people around them.

There is a mistrust of others which arises out of not feeling worthy of love, so even if they are shown genuine signs of affection by others they will have difficulty in accepting this at face value. By the same token, a constant need for reassurance is also frequently present in those with low self-esteem.

Put simply, if I have high self-esteem I can accept praise for what I do right, but I'm also receptive to constructive criticism so I can learn from what I do wrong. If I have low self-esteem I find myself unable to believe the compliments I receive but may also blame others for any failures in my life. They do this as a defence mechanism, because secretly they believe any misfortunes they encounter to be entirely their own fault.

Some outwards signs of high self-esteem would be self-direction, non-blaming behaviour and an awareness of personal strengths and limitations. People with high self-esteem have an ability to make mistakes and learn from them. They won't dwell on 'what could have been' and beat themselves up for missing an opportunity and in the same way they can also accept mistakes in others without blame.

'I think self-esteem is something you can train your brain into learning. Like walking or talking, I believe it is important to teach children from an early age that they are of value.' *Victoria, 22*

People with high self-esteem generally have the ability to socialise in groups of any size but they are also, crucially, equally content to be in their own company (although it should be noted here that there are other personality types/mental illnesses that might make it difficult for a person to socialise, or equally hate being alone). They have an inner peace which means they can be alone without being lonely and are not tortured by their own thoughts. They will always try to solve a problem on their own initially but, if they cannot, they have the ability to ask for help from others without assuming that this makes them weak or inadequate in any way. This makes them both co-operative and independent.

If you have high self-esteem you will be comfortable with the word 'no'. You won't follow the crowd if you believe something to be wrong and you'll be confident enough to express your reasons and risk upsetting the people around you. However, it's likely that you'll still be popular because you'll be naturally optimistic and we are drawn to positive people.

People with high self-esteem will be able to handle a range of different feelings. They know that, whatever they feel, it is okay to feel that way. By the same token, however, they won't hold onto that feeling for long periods of time. They'll experience the emotion, let it go and move on.

'I believe self-esteem is definitely a learned behaviour. It is something that can be built on and improved. I feel it helps if this is encouraged from a young age, however self-esteem can be improved at any time by having a more positive and realistic outlook on life.' *Lily, 17*

High self-esteem goes hand in hand with a positive image of oneself, both emotionally and physically. If you feel you are of value to yourself, others and to the world you are more likely to take care of your body and your health. This is a delicate one to detect from the outside, because whilst a person with low self-esteem might, for example, go the gym because they hate the way they look and want to change it, a person with high self-esteem will still go to the gym, because they want to work out to build strength and remain healthy. It's why people undertake health and beauty regimes that is the important thing to examine, not what they do.

So you can see how the amount of self-esteem we have permeates every aspect of our lives. When people think of 'self-esteem' they usually associate it with romantic relationships and friendships. Whilst it is an incredibly important part of this arena, it will also affect how we think and behave at school, university or in a working environment, as well as directly impacting our physical health. It will determine what we believe we are capable of, the decisions that we do or do not make and the risks we are prepared to take.

Positive self-esteem gives us the strength and flexibility to take charge of our lives and grow from our mistakes without the fear of rejection.

'I think that people with high self-esteem are very confident in themselves, how they look and how they are. They don't worry about what other people think of them.' *Amy, 19*

Natasha

Back in the early days of my self-esteem teaching a student accosted me in the hall after class, all wild-eyed with desperation, asking me to tell her '*What the secret to being confident is*'.

Further investigation uncovered the fact that this particular young woman had to stand up in front of her class to do a presentation, for the very first time, that afternoon. She'd seen me 'do public speaking' in front of her year group and figured, quite reasonably, that I knew some significant universal truth which she did not.

After that incident, I started noticing a lot of people who seemed to be labouring under this particular misapprehension. Somehow, people who feel that they are lacking in confidence have gleaned the idea that the people who exude the stuff have been let into a 'secret'. Following this logic, if they can only learn said secret then – TA DAAA! – they will become instantaneously confident too.

I had to explain to the student in question (and everyone else since) that, unfortunately, confidence doesn't work like that. It is a truth universally acknowledged that the first time we do anything new the chances are that we will shit ourselves. The unknown is always frightening, simply by virtue of being unknown.

Cast your mind back to your first day at school or work. Or the first time you took public transport by yourself, or tried to drive a car, or introduced yourself into a new environment, or went on a date. Remember how pant-wettingly terrifying it was? If you are an adult of, let's say, twenty-five or over, you'll probably have had to do one or all of those things squillions of times by now. You probably think nothing of hopping on a train or jumping in your car to go to work and nattering away with merry abandon to your colleagues about the blind date you went on last night. Crucially, you are now *confident* about doing all of those activities.

'Confidence' and 'practice' are, in my humble opinion, exactly the same thing. If you practice something often enough it becomes second nature and any accompanying scariness evaporates. The first time I had to stand up and speak in assembly (at eleven years old) I remember distinctly that I very nearly passed out and vomited all over myself. Today, I speak to hundreds of assemblies, of *teenagers* no less (the hardest-to-impress demographic in the known universe) and think nothing of being under the scrutiny of a thousand pairs of eyes with an innate propensity for piss-take-age, because I've done it so many times.

I find taking this ethos and applying it to self-esteem incredibly helpful for the mind-set. It makes self-esteem seem less vague, ethereal and elusive. Everyone is capable of making the effort to practice thinking in positive ways. If you're able to do it until thinking positively becomes second nature then what you're left with is high self-esteem. Of course that's an awful lot easier said than done but the theory, at least, is a simple one.

In the same way, so-called 'lack-of' self-esteem isn't, in fact, an absence of anything. People who lack self-esteem are actively making themselves feel terrible, every second they're conscious. It's known as 'being self-critical' in psychological circles but I prefer to call it 'self-bashing'. We all have an inner monologue, a tiny voice in the recess of our mind that chatters away incessantly as we go about our days. For some that voice is a cheerleader, saying '*Yay! Go you! You can totally do this!*' For others, the voice tells them they are worthless and inferior to the people around them. The art of gaining self-esteem is essentially the act of telling the latter voice to shut up and replacing it with the former one.

There are various ways people have found throughout history to achieve this. You will most likely find it is a question of trial and error until you find a self-esteem building exercise that sits well with the way you think.

Some people find 'affirmations', which are positive statements one repeats to oneself several times each day, fantastically helpful and life-changing. Other people try it and feel like a complete tit. You have to cast aside your inhibitions (or, in my case, instinct to laugh) and have a go in order to see with which camp you dwell. (Hint: in my experience, the trick is to come up with an affirmation which is something akin to the language you already use when you speak normally. There is absolutely no point in repeating '*I am a Magnificent Empress of Wonder*' in front of the mirror twenty times each morning if your instant reaction to hearing that sentence is '*idiot*'. An affirmation I quite like for its universal qualities is '*I am good enough*' – simple, effective and reassuringly British, in that it doesn't seem too much like boasting).

For others 'anchoring' to a moment when they felt particularly good about themselves is the key to overcoming self-esteem wobbles. Changing the words used in everyday conversation in the home and at school can also facilitate the creation of new patterns of language in the brain. For body confidence, pinpointing body parts we feel positive about to look at first when we see our reflection can be a powerful exercise. Creating a 'character' – a more confident version of the current self – to 'inhabit' at times when feeling intimidated has been indescribably valuable for a lot of shy students I've worked with. Breathing exercises which 'bring us into the moment' are brilliant, as is getting your best friend to write all the things they like about you on post-its and then stick them all over your clothes until you resemble a cartoon duck. Some of these exercises and practices will be described in more detail later in the book.

The old adage says it takes three days to create a habit and three weeks to break it. According to NLP, it's actually more like three months to completely let go of an old habit and recreate a new one. Dedicate yourself to repeating new and unfamiliar ways of speaking, thinking and looking for three months and you **will** start to feel different – for the science tells us it is so. Not only that, but *clichéd sentence ahoy but I can't think how else to say it, sorry* positive people project positivity thereby making others around them feel more positive too.

If you are a parent or teacher, just practising these behaviours yourself will impact your environment and that's before you've even encouraged the young people you're surrounded with to try it themselves.

There is of course another way to describe all this – 'fake it 'til you make it'. That, in the Gospel-according-to-me, is what 'the secret to being confident is'.

CHAPTER 2

WHAT IS MENTAL ILLNESS?

SIGNS, SYMPTOMS AND INTUITION

Lynn

Before I begin to describe some of the signs and symptoms and what we should look for when it comes to mental illness, it's important to remember that this chapter will not be completely exhaustive. Human beings are so diverse and varied, it would be impossible to write a book that encompassed everyone's experiences.

Below are some general guidelines designed to help you to determine when the line is crossed between common-or-garden teenage angst and what could develop into something more worrying. However, parents and carers who regularly spend time with young people know them better than anyone else. There really is no substitute for intuition. If you feel that there is something 'amiss' with a young person you know then there is likely to be a good reason for that instinct. We have gut feelings for a purpose.

I have described in detail the five most common mental illnesses experienced by the young. Although each mental illness has its own characteristics, they are often intertwined and tend to 'borrow' symptoms from one another.

WHAT IS MENTAL ILLNESS?

A mental illness can be defined as a health condition that changes a person's way of thinking, their feelings, their behaviour, or all three. This causes the person distress and difficulty in functioning mentally, and frequently on a physical level too. Individuals who have a mental illness may not look as though they are sick, particularly if their symptoms are mild. Other individuals may show more obvious and explicit physical signs.

It's important to remember that it is natural to feel happy when something positive or good happens and to feel sad or angry when something negative happens. It's equally normal to experience fear and anxiety when dealing with a worrying event. Part of ensuring good mental health and wellbeing is being able to recognise that it is natural to feel different feelings and emotions. Good mental health does not mean being happy all the time. It's crucial to learn and recognise when we are reacting to something, or when prolonged feelings indicate a potential problem.

Mental illness can affect a wide variety of different people. The impact varies from person to person, as does the length of time it will affect each person's life.

Although mental illnesses are just as serious and deserve the same attention and respect as physical illness, they are often misunderstood and feared because they cannot be seen. If we were to break one of our legs, not only would a doctor know exactly how to fix it, but we'd probably get a lot of sympathy and support from the people around us. With a mental illness, there is no such obvious 'cure' and people around the sufferer tend to draw away, or worry that they will say the wrong thing. This can be frustrating for someone experiencing mental illness, as they might feel that their condition has not been acknowledged or that the people close to them do not care.

Mental illnesses can be quite secretive, in addition to being lonely, and are often accompanied by feelings of shame. Because of their illusive nature, it's difficult to quantify and measure mental illness. I would be inclined to measure their severity by looking at the impact on the life of the person experiencing the illness and those of the people around them. Can they concentrate in school? Can they hold down a job? Can they socialise? Can they maintain friendships and romantic relationships? Are they sleeping? Are they looking after their body? All of these can be negatively affected by mental illness to a huge extent.

ANXIETY

Not only is anxiety the commonest form of mental illness in the Western world, it is also how many other mental illness begin. Symptoms of anxiety permeate every other form of mental illness.

Anxiety has a strong effect, because it is part of our evolution. The 'flight or fight' response to potentially dangerous situations is what allowed our ancestors to hunt and protect themselves from physical danger. Stress and anxiety are the emotions that are supposed to accompany these physical instincts. It causes the mind and body to speed up to allow us to react. It will also push out any other thoughts, dominating the mind. In today's world, where there are no wildebeest to wrestle, we are simply left with a heightened sense of unease.

However, today's life is full of stressful situations and events and it's normal to feel a certain amount of anxiety attributable to these everyday events. The difference with Generalised Anxiety Disorder (GAD), which is the technical term for prolonged anxiety, is that the sufferer will find it almost impossible to control and contextualise these worries.

The physical signs of GAD during an episode of severe anxiety include:

Rapid and/or irregular heartbeat
Fast breathing
Sweating
Dizziness
Dry mouth
Churning stomach
Loose bowels.

The psychological impact tends to occur after the episode and is likely to include:

Lack of concentration
Feeling irritable
Lack of patience
Feeling low/depressed
Drowsiness/tiredness
A sense of apathy
Loss of confidence.

A highly anxious person is likely to develop coping mechanisms, which might actually take them into the territory of a different mental illness. It's difficult to cite a mental illness that doesn't begin with feelings of anxiety and if these emotions are exacerbated then they may develop into any of the following:

OBSESSIVE COMPULSIVE DISORDER (OCD)

As the name suggests, this disorder is formed of two distinct parts – obsession and compulsion. Intrusive thoughts form the mental aspect of the condition and these thoughts often give way to compulsive (or repetitive) behaviours.

Most of us have worries, doubts and superstitious beliefs of some kind. It is only when your thoughts and actions make no sense to others, become excessive or begin to impact your ability to live a normal life and to affect people around the sufferer that it is officially recognised as a condition. Many people have described themselves as 'a little bit OCD' when what they really mean is that they like to keep their house clean and tidy or have a very organised filing system, for example. Neither of these are characteristics of the illness if they are in a manageable form. It's important to recognise the distinction between 'OCD' as a generalised slang term and the medical condition, which can be totally debilitating.

Some people experience intrusive thoughts, but do not have the desire to carry out compulsive actions. However, much of the time the two components will go hand in hand.

Obsessions are involuntary, seemingly uncontrollable thoughts, images or impulses which occur over and over in the mind. A person experiencing intrusive thoughts will not invite these thoughts or enjoy having them, but cannot seem to stop them from invading their mind. Some people describe these thoughts as being 'like a stuck record' and just as irritating, yet actively trying to stop them can, perversely, make them worse.

Compulsions are behaviours or rituals that must be acted out again and again. Usually, compulsions are performed in an attempt to make obsession go away. For example, if you are afraid of germs and cannot seem to think about anything else, you might develop elaborate cleaning rituals. However, the relief is short lived. In fact, the obsessive thoughts will usually come back stronger.

In its simplest form, OCD occurs in a four-step pattern:

1. Obsession – The mind is overwhelmed with a constant obsessive fear or concern, such as one's house being burgled.

2. Anxiety – The obsession provokes a feeling of intense anxiety and distress, often causing the 'worst case scenario' to be envisaged or imagined, sometimes repeatedly.

3. Compulsions – A pattern of compulsive behaviour is adopted in an attempt to reduce the anxiety and distress, such as checking all windows and doors are locked three times before leaving the house or going to bed.

4. Temporary relief – Compulsive behaviour brings transitory belief from anxiety.

Obsession or anxiety will almost always return after the above cycle has been completed, causing it to start all over again. Compulsive behaviours in themselves can often result in anxiety, as they become more time consuming and start to demand more and more time. Anxiety can manifest itself in obsessive thoughts and so the condition spirals.

It's difficult to give a definitive list of signs and symptoms of OCD, since there are infinite things that can trigger an obsession and to behave accordingly. Some of the commonest obsessions are:

Fear of being contaminated by germs or dirt, or of contaminating others.

Fear of causing harm to yourself or others.

Intrusive sexual, explicit or violent thoughts or recurrent images.

Obsessive focus on religious or moral ideas.

Fear of losing or not having things that may be needed.

Order and symmetry – the idea that all physical objects must line up 'just so'.

Special attention to something considered lucky or unlucky ('superstitions').

The commonest forms of compulsive behaviour are:

Counting, tapping, repeating certain words or doing other seemingly senseless things in an attempt to reduce anxiety.

Spending a lot of time washing or cleaning, either the body or the environment.

Repeatedly checking in on loved-ones to ensure that they are safe.

Excessive double-checking of locks, appliances and switches.

Ordering or arranging objects into specific orders.

Praying or engaging in rituals triggered by religious fear to an excessive extent.

Accumulating junk such as old newspapers or empty food containers.

Without adequate coping mechanisms, OCD can eat into so much of a person's life that they find themselves unable to do anything else. This can result in extensive difficulties at home, school and work.

SELF-HARM

Self-harm in the most literal sense of the word is when a person chooses to inflict harm on their body. It is often undertaken as a way of dealing with very difficult or complicated feelings.

'Classic' ways of self-harming include deliberately cutting and burning the skin, however there are less obvious forms of self-harm, such as purposefully putting oneself in risky situations or exercising to the point of pain. Eating disorders could also be described as a form of self-harm, since it broadly encompasses anything that is done to the physical self in an attempt to deal with or block out what is happening in the mind.

Like compulsive behaviours, self-harm is designed to bring about a feeling of relief and in just the same way the respite is temporary. These behaviours can also be both physically and mentally addictive.

*Self-harm, like so many mental illnesses, has been completely transformed by the existence of the internet. We tend to think of self-harmers as being very secretive and ashamed of their behaviours, covering up in clothing that will hide any resultant scars or abrasions. Yet there is now an online community of people brought together by self-harm and these people often see scars as 'badges of honour' which signify their membership to that club. We cannot assume that a self-harmer will always cover up their behaviours, but we must always keep in mind that not all the signs of self-harm are immediately obvious, either. **I cannot stress enough that self-harm, as with any mental condition, differs wildly from person to person.***

Some of the signs of self-harm are explained as an 'accident'. A self-harmer might claim they fell over, for example, to justify a bruise. So actually the most important indicator of self-harm is the frequency and persistency of injuries, which mean they are no longer a feasible 'one off'.

Some of the physical signs to look out for would include:

> *Bruises*
>
> *Cigarette burns*
>
> *Cuts*
>
> *Excessive hair loss/unexplained patches in the scalp*
>
> *Exercising obsessively (considerably more than the recommended amount of half an hour per day)*
>
> *Keeping covered with layers of clothing, especially long sleeves, at all times (even in hot weather)*
>
> *Low mood/tearfulness/lack of motivation or interest*
>
> *Changes in eating habits or being secretive about eating, including any unusual/rapid weight loss or gain*
>
> *Alcohol or drug misuse.*

Self-harm statistically affects men and women equally. Whilst teenage girls often use self-harm as a physical expression of familiar yet painful emotions, teenage boys are likely to self-harm because they don't have the emotional vocabulary to express how they feel. Self-harm can be a way of seeking attention, physicalising an internal pain for the outside world to see in a way that demands action. It can also be an indicator of suicidal thoughts, allowing the self-harmer to 'test the waters' without having to go so far as to take their own life.

In conclusion, self-harm is an indicator of an emotional issue that requires attention and it's almost always recommended that intervention takes place as quickly as possible after the signs are noticed. Self-harm has also been noted to be 'contagious', with teachers describing 'epidemics' happening within their schools. It's therefore a good idea to ensure that friends of the self-harmer know intervention is taking place, giving the message that this is a serious condition and one that should not be emulated.

DEPRESSION

Depression is a common condition that causes extended periods of low mood, loss of interest in things the sufferer once found pleasurable, feelings of guilt or low self-worth, disturbed sleep or appetite, low energy or poor concentration.

Depression is different from simply feeling 'down' or sad. Unhappiness is something that everyone feels at one time or another, usually due to a specific cause. A person suffering from depression will experience intense anxiety, hopelessness, despair, negativity and helplessness and the feelings stay with them instead of subsiding over time.

Depression can happen to anyone. Many successful, wealthy and/or intelligent people who may appear to the outside world to 'have everything' battle with this condition. By its very nature, depression is not a logical reaction to the things around the person suffering from it, so it does not matter how many material possessions, friends or loved ones that person might have.

Half the people who experience an episode of depression will only go through it once. For the other half, there will be recurring incidences of depression throughout their lives. Living with depression can be incredibly difficult for the person experiencing it and frustrating for the people around them. People with depression often cannot see that they are depressed, even when it is pointed out to them, because depression has distorted their perception.

Depression can arise out of low self-esteem, anxiety, OCD or an eating disorder, or indeed it can be the root cause of one of the aforementioned conditions. It is 'chicken and egg'.

Signs and symptoms of depression include:

   Tiredness and loss of energy

   Sadness that does not go away

   Loss of self-confidence

   Difficulty in concentrating

   Avoiding other people, even close friends and family

   Not being able to enjoy activities that are usually pleasurable

   Feeling anxious constantly

   Insomnia – difficulty in 'drifting off' or waking much earlier than usual

   Feelings of helplessness and hopelessness

   Very strong feelings of guilt or worthlessness

   Finding it hard to function at school or work

   Changes in appetite, resulting in weight loss or gain

   Loss of sex drive

   Physical aches and pains

   Self-harm and suicidal thoughts.

It's worth noting here that saying things like 'no one understands me!' and 'I wish I'd never been born!' are classic parts of the journey experienced by most teenagers as they grow up. Temper tantrums are inevitable at a time when the body is swimming with hormones. The most important sign to look out for is general demeanour. If, for example, a teenager says they hate the world, but then precedes to go and kick a ball around in the sunshine with their friends, they probably aren't depressed. Prolonged apathy is the cornerstone of depression, as is feeling that everyone else's life is somehow better.

EATING DISORDERS

Eating disorders are ways people find to abuse food, exercise and their bodies but they originate and are characterised by disordered thinking and mental distress. Like self-harm, eating disorders are a physical manifestation of something that is happening within the brain and effects on the body are merely symptoms. Eating disorders cannot be measured in stones and pounds, but are instead about feelings and behaviours.

Eating disorders frequently co-exist with other mental illness. They have been linked to alcoholism and drug addiction, have strong links with OCD, anxiety, self-harm and depression. The condition may begin with simply eating too little or too much, but obsession with eating, exercise and, often, body image takes over, leading to severe changes in the way the sufferer lives and behaves.

There are many types of eating disorders and within these types there are hundreds of variations in symptoms. Whilst there are some common themes that unite all eating disorders, like low self-esteem, most of the illness are 'tailored' to the sufferer. The three most well-known eating disorders are anorexia, bulimia and compulsive eating disorder, which are described below, yet the most common actual diagnosis is 'EDNOS' (Eating Disorder Not Otherwise Specified) which means that the patient does not completely fit with the official criteria for one eating disorder in particular.

Anorexia Nervosa

The official definition of anorexia is 'self-imposed starvation'. However, anorexia is not really about how little a person eats, it's about their desire to control what they eat. Anorexics know exactly how much they will eat in a day, at what times they will eat and often count how many calories they are consuming. They will often weigh and measure their food and are likely to become fearful in situations where they have to deviate from the food plan they have set for themselves.

An anorexic will go to great lengths to eat according to the rules their illness tells them are necessary. They will hide their behaviour, lie to their loved ones and engage in morally questionable behaviours which prioritise their condition above anything and anyone else in their lives.

Signs of anorexia, which will help distinguish anorexia from a diet or phase are below. It's important to note that usually there's more than one sign, although that isn't always the case:

Avoidance of food and meal times

Making repeated excuses to avoid eating, such as having 'eaten earlier'

Picking out a few specific foods and eating these in very small quantities

Carefully weighing and portioning food

Checking calories and fat content of food

Keeping lists of food consumed

Denying hunger

Hiding food that you were led to believe had been eaten

Intense and compulsive exercise

Continual self-effacing language, such as repeatedly claiming to be 'fat'

Continually looking for approval and validation

Physical signs of anorexia:

Rapid weight loss

Dizzy spells/feeling faint

Constipation and stomach pain

'Langugo' – soft, downy hair on the face and body

Hair loss on the scalp

Poor circulation and feeling cold (particularly on the hands, nose and feet)

Dry, rough or discoloured skin

In girls, periods stop or do not start in the first place

Dehydration

The physical symptoms above usually clear up once the sufferer enters into recovery, however it is important to note that they are at risk of long-term health consequences, such as osteoporosis and infertility.

Bulimia

Bulimia nervosa can be just as serious as anorexia and yet is more difficult to detect from the outside, since sufferers are quite often a 'normal' weight, or even slightly overweight.

People who have bulimia continually 'binge', eating large quantities of food in a short period of time, and then 'purge', finding ways to rid their body of the food consumed, most commonly by vomiting. In my experience, it's becoming increasingly common for people to purge using excessive exercise, too. Like anorexics, bulimics will sometimes go through periods of starvation and this is also a means of 'purging' or compensating for having eaten large amounts previously. There is a diagnosis of 'anorexia, bulimia subtype' and this is when anorexics 'purge', but it is the consumption of large quantities of food that is the defining factor that distinguishes bulimia as the primary diagnosis.

Signs of bulimia include:

Urges to eat large amounts of food

Mood swings

Anxiety and depression

Constantly putting themselves down

Feeling ashamed or guilty

Vomiting after eating

Use of laxatives

Compulsive exercise

Secrecy and reluctance to socialise

Effects of bulimia on the body:

Sore throat

Tooth decay/acid erosion

Bad breath (or constantly chewing gum to compensate for bad breath)

Dry or patchy skin

Irregular periods

Tiredness

Redness around the knuckles

Puffiness of face and fingers

Compulsive and Binge Eating

This has only been recognised as an official eating disorder fairly recently. It's an important step forward, because when people overeat we don't tend to have as much sympathy for them as those who starve themselves, even though the effects on the body and mind can be just as harmful.

People with compulsive and overeating disorder suffer from episodes of uncontrolled eating or binging, followed by guilt and depression, although they do not then purge. In addition to eating large quantities of food, the sufferer will also usually have a 'frenzied' feeling as though they are unable to control their actions. They may continue to eat long after they have become full.

Signs of binge/compulsive eating:

Fear of not being able to control eating and/or not being able to stop eating

Fear of eating around others

Believing that life would be better if they were able to lose weight

Putting themselves down, especially after eating

Blaming personal failures in social and professional life on their weight

Depression/mood swings

Fatigue

Sporadic use of popular diet plans

Hiding food in secret places to eat later

Secretive eating patterns.

Effects of binge eating/compulsive eating on the body:

Weight gain

Becoming out of breath after light activity

Excessive sweating

High blood pressure and/or cholesterol

Leg and joint pain

Decreased mobility owing to weight gain

Loss of sexual desire

Insomnia

Poor sleeping habits.

It's important to note here that it is possible to binge eat or eat compulsively and not be overweight. However, this is still a *problem, both physically and mentally. Our health is dictated not by how much we weigh, but by how much fat is around our internal organs. It is possible to be a small size and have unseen fat around the heart and arteries. Using food as a kind of drug is also not healthy emotionally. There is a difference between this and simply having a 'high metabolism' or 'large appetite'.*

CONCLUSION

Mental illness will statistically affect 25 per cent of the population and so it is important that we understand these conditions. There is still a lot of stigma surrounding mental illness, yet with the right approach and treatment they can in most cases be managed and the sufferer can go on to live a happy and fulfilling life.

Natasha

If you are very, very lucky, a person will come into your life who forces you to completely rethink your understanding of mental illness and our cultural attitudes towards it. In my case, that person is my best friend, Grace Barrett.

I first met Grace in 2009 when I was sent – under considerable duress – by one of my editors to review an open mic night in Archway, North London. As anticipated, it wasn't the most transcendent evening of musical entertainment I've ever witnessed. The acts all seemed to fit into the same tedious mould, warbling tunelessly around the actual notes of the ACTUAL song, clearly believing themselves to be Mariah Carey. I was just about to reconcile myself to the fact that my subsequent review would be four words long (reading *'they were all shit'*), neck my rum and coke and peg it home, when the most intriguing woman bounced onto the stage.

She was wearing a green silk backless jumpsuit and had the biggest Afro I'd ever seen in my entire life. She was probably the most gorgeous human I'd seen in the flesh, yet seemed refreshingly unbothered by her own beauty, greeting the audience with her broad Northern twang and a gigantic, infectious grin. As she began her set (which was, according to my later review *'what would happen if Massive Attack's 'Dissolved Girl' had a baby with Kelis' 'I hate you so much right now' and therefore, naturally, brilliant'*), it suddenly dawned on me that I **needed** this woman in my life.

The thought remained potent and persistent, even the next day when the rum had worn off. So, I got her email address from the event organisers under the guise of some journalism-related reason and proceeded to keep inviting her to things. Plays, showcases, events with free booze and nibbles – basically any time my press invite had a 'plus one' I dropped her an email. I learned that it was literally impossible to be in a bad mood when Grace was around. She was (and continues to be) an unusual combination of completely down to earth, terrifyingly insightful and astonishingly optimistic. I basked in the sunshine she emitted.

One day it occurred to me that there wasn't anything on the foreseeable horizon I could invite Grace to and simply asked her, outright *'shall we be friends?'* Instead of saying *'No, you weirdo, you're clearly stalking me and I'm only in it for the free champagne'* she simply said *'Yeah, go on then'*. We've been best friends ever since and can often be found eating tapas whilst rendered utterly floppy and helpless with laughter over something no one else on the planet could possibly understand.

Getting to know Grace away from her stage persona, which is a kind of hyper-sexual, uber-energetic version of the 'real' her, has made me realise that, in the words of the Wizard in Disney's *Sword in the Stone* '*for every high there is a low*'. Grace sometimes experiences periods of intense paranoia and sadness. She also has a condition called 'synaesthesia', which is where the brain's neural pathways become confused, so that noises can be experienced as tastes or, in Grace's case, colours. (Apparently my speaking voice is '*a sort of warm, rusty red*'. Which is nice.)

Crucially, however, the huge spectrum of human emotions Grace is able to tune into, combined with her ability to 'hear' colours and see sound is part of what makes her so creative, musically. And making music, in addition to being her all-consuming *raison d'etre*, is what pulls her out of her funk (excuse the pun) whenever she is having a 'down' day. Which would present quite the conundrum, were she to consider it requisite to 'cure' herself of her 'mental illness'. She prefers, instead, to live within the confines of her slightly peculiar but wonderful mind, in the way that nature intended.

When I asked Grace to explain it in her own words she said:

I'd rather deal with the extras that are sometimes very negative than lose the trippy little stained glass window that I see the world through on the good and bad days. It's the thing that gives me most joy ... that's why I try to make noises for a living. Taking the edge off that in order to take the edge off the bad days would be, I think, like living my whole life in a soft-walled room painted magnolia – very safe but very boring!

I have absolutely no doubt that, if Grace didn't have a 'mental illness', she would be less 'Grace'. She'd lose the spark that drew me to her, in that dingy bar in Archway all those years ago. She would be robbed of her inherent Grace-ness. Yet – and here is the important bit – she always knows when she is having an 'episode' and has developed non-medicinal coping mechanisms which allow her to live her life as a fully functional human being. She's in regular contact with a GP who understands her needs and hasn't ruled out the possibility of taking medication if her symptoms ever begin to overwhelm her. Thus, her 'mental illness' stops being an 'illness' and merely becomes 'the way Grace thinks which is different from the status quo'.

Having Grace as a permanent and regular fixture in my life has meant attempting to understand what it is like within the confines of her brain, something which is invariably exciting rather than scary. It has also completely transformed the way I think about mental 'illness'.

The way I see it, if I was locked in a room with any other person for long enough I would eventually end up thinking they were a lunatic. Everyone thinks in their own unique and distinctive way, it's just that some people's way of thinking more closely resembles what we as a society consider 'acceptable' and 'normal' than others.

The term 'mental illness' in itself is, I would argue, stigmatising and part of the reason there continues to be so much stigma surrounding those conditions which are described using that term. There is not one of the symptoms Lynn has detailed above as being symptomatic of mental illness that I cannot personally relate to in some way. I have at various points throughout my life felt anxious, lonely, depressed; I have felt unexplained compulsions to behave irrationally; I have thought about harming myself. If you haven't at any stage experienced these emotions at least fleetingly then that would, I'd argue, make you highly unusual.

The problem with our incessant human need to label each other is that a diagnosis of mental illness can become the sum total of the way a person is perceived. As a society we need to understand that whilst a mental illness is undoubtedly part of a person, either temporarily or permanently, it does not define who they are. Mental illnesses are automatically associated with irrational behaviour and unpredictability, and that can make them a lonely experience. Previous friends can begin to avoid those with diagnosed conditions, fearing for their own safety, which is ironic when you consider that for most people diagnosis marks the point when they begin to understand themselves better and take control over their own behaviour.

We all have quirks, eccentricities and illogical insecurities. The key questions are:

1. Is the way I'm thinking and behaving stopping me from functioning effectively?

2. Am I harming/distressing either myself or the people around me?

If the answer to either or both of these questions is 'yes' then you need some help and guidance to see you through this period of difficulty. But you still won't be 'normal' at the end of the process, because 'normal' doesn't really exist. It's really difficult to even define optimum mental health, let alone achieve it.

'Normal' is merely a social construct by which we measure something which is almost infinitely diverse – the human condition. Trying to be 'normal', therefore, is a fruitless and counter-productive endeavour.

You can only ever strive to be the best version of yourself.

INTERVIEW WITH LUCIE RUSSELL
DIRECTOR OF CAMPAIGNS AND MEDIA, YOUNG MINDS

Natasha

I love Lucie Russell.

Quite often, when you're speaking with people who work for charities they're very knowledgeable about their subject but you can just tell they don't REALLY care. They're doing the rounds, being *insert job title here* within various charities, covering a huge spectrum of health and social issues and (reasonably I suppose) simply don't have enough room in their heads to care deeply about everything that has come under their jurisdiction, throughout their careers.

Lucie is the antithesis of that. She cares so much you think her head is going to fall off. The conversations we've had have been characterised either by her ranting in my direction or me ranting in her direction and whoever isn't ranting is nodding vehemently and frothing at the mouth, slightly. Really, someone should take a picture of us and put it online somewhere to be recalled whenever anyone asks for the official definition of 'putting the world to rights'.

When this book is published, Lynn and I are going to make a donation to Young Minds (we were going to give a percentage of each book sale but, owing to cuts to funding, at the time of writing Young Minds are in danger of having their Parent Helpline closed and are in need of expedient dosh). In addition to providing training services for professionals and support for young people and their carers, Young Minds campaign to ensure the voices of the youth of this country are not ignored when it comes to mental health issues. Their work is crucial and, as an organisation, they rock.

So here is my interview with Lucie, who is Director of Campaigns and Media and who you will start to see on the telly all the time, now that you know her name:

Q: What are the commonest mental health struggles faced by people under twenty-one, in Britain?
without hesitation *Anxiety, self-harm, conduct disorder and eating disorders.*

Q: What exactly is 'conduct disorder'?
It's any sort of behavioural problem, so what we might call 'acting out', aggression, shouting or being difficult at school. It's generally behaving in an anti-social way.

Q: Is that a thing in its own right, or is it more likely to be a symptom of another condition?
It's both. It's absolutely a condition in its own right and it doesn't have to be a symptom of anything else. Having said that, it's also often related to ADHD (Attention Deficit Hyperactivity Disorder) and Aspergers Syndrome.

Q: Do you think the support out there for young people with mental health issues is sufficient?

laughs in a derisory way *Absolutely not. Statutory children and young people's mental health services are being cut drastically and have been for (many) years.*

There are four tiers to CAMHS (Child and Adolescent Mental Health Services). Tiers one and two are universal services, so for example counsellors and support workers in schools, educational psychologists and parenting programmes. These are funded by the local authority and have been drastically cut.

Tiers three and four are services you would be referred for, so psychiatry services and in-patient units etc. and they are also being cut. Young people who are suffering are often not being picked up by specialist services, so their problems are getting worse and becoming more entrenched.

Even the mental health services that ARE available are often not very child-friendly. If and when a young person does get referred it is often an alienating experience. They tend to end up not carrying on and get lost in the system.

The other problem is transition – when young people are sixteen, if they are getting CAMHS services they transition into adult services, but adult services have a higher threshold than CAMHS, so many young people slip through the net at this point.

There is an ongoing issue surrounding whose responsibility it is to support young people. Ultimately, everyone who works with children and young people needs to have an understanding of how to assist them in developing good mental health and how to help people who are struggling. Despite this, there is no compulsory component on mental health in teacher training. Teachers learn through CPD (Continuing Professional Development), which is voluntary. GP mental health training is only a tiny component, also, which seems illogical when you consider one in every four GP visits is for a mental health problem. A lot of parents don't really understand how to foster good mental health in their children, either.

So no, I don't think support is sufficient. Young people are being failed on a number of levels.

Q: How do mental health issues manifest differently in young people to adults?
Oooh. I've never been asked that before. Good question.
waves hand dismissively whilst feeling secretly very pleased
Thanks.
The illnesses themselves are the same in young people and adults – the difference is because you are younger you don't 'get it' in the same way because you don't have the same understanding you have when you're an adult. Young people often think the mental health issues they're experiencing are normal or maybe that they're just part and parcel of growing up. They have no basis for comparison. They haven't felt adult and 'normal' yet.

The way a young person will react to an emerging mental health problem may be very different to an adult as well. They might refuse to go to school because of anxiety, for example.

Young people are much more likely to be ridiculed for having a mental health problem, once it's been identified, too. In teenage years they are very likely to try and self-medicate with drink and drugs.

Q: A big dilemma for parents and teachers is the tipping point for concern and intervention – at what point can they say with authority this isn't just 'growing up' but is a recognised mental health issue?

It's really all about extent – locking yourself in your room and shouting at your parents or generally being a pain in the arse once in a while is part of being a teenager. Staying in your room all the time or not sleeping a lot or perhaps being consistently aggressive, isolating yourself and not being able to socialise on frequent occasions – these are the signs that something might be wrong. It's how often they are doing something, rather than what they do, which differentiates. When something is happening all the time, there is something not right. Refusing to go to school is also a recurring theme.

Q: How do adults go about talking about mental health with young people?

It's all about how you frame it. Don't start off by using the phrase 'mental illness'. Ask them instead how they are feeling. Acknowledge that growing up is really hard and scary and can be very confusing, but that opening up and communicating about how you feel makes it a lot easier. It's important that the young person doesn't feel judged or that you are trying to diagnose them.

There's still so much stigma surrounding mental illness – especially amongst young people – and it makes the 'them and us' mentality even worse. You don't want them to come away from the conversation feeling that they're not okay and everyone else is. You need to reach out on their level.

You might want to talk about your own experience when you were young, stressing that whatever they're going through isn't abnormal.

Finally, spell it out that you are there for them and that you will help them get the help that they need.

Q: How do parents deal with stigma and prejudice from other adults?
The worst thing if someone you love has a mental health issue is the feeling that it's your fault. We think everything is our fault; it's the eternal position of a parent! You also believe that everyone else will think it's your fault, too, and that makes you not want to tell anyone else....But what you will find is that if you do talk about it most parents are going through something similar.

Ultimately, though, you can't be responsible for other people's responses. The more we don't talk about mental health the more taboo it gets and the more families can't support each other. Most of the time you aren't being judged in the way that you think you are, but if you do encounter prejudice and judgement, well, that's their problem, not yours.

Q: What sorts of things are you hearing from people who ring your parent helpline and what advice do you give?
Parents who ring our helpline often say they feel they have failed – they don't feel in control of their family anymore and want to know what they have done wrong. They used to have a little kid who they could tell what to do and now they have a teenager who they can't control.

The commonest question we get asked is about behaviour: How do I manage my child's behaviour? Parents often feel disempowered. A lot of the time their children are harming themselves or being aggressive to their own families and they want to know how they can get hold of this behaviour, in a practical way.

*Usually, they have forgotten that they **are** in control and that they're running things, not the child. With teenagers, they're becoming independent and the conflict about who is in charge is a really big issue within the household. That's normal and natural, but it's crucial to keep in mind the fact that you are in control, not them.*

We help parents find ways of getting that control back again, like setting boundaries and sticking to them. Sometimes, you have to risk being unpopular. Young people feel unsafe if they don't have boundaries.

If we think the problems are so bad they might need some other input from children's mental health services, we can refer them.

A lot of what happens to the child is a reflection of the dynamics of the family being displaced on the child. The stresses and strains on the family and what their child is exhibiting are likely to be linked. So if you can get to the root of what's happening within that family, the behaviours of the young person quite often disappear.

CHAPTER 3

SELF-ESTEEM IN FAMILIES

Lynn

'Peers and family can help with improving your self-esteem and boosting your overall confidence. Subtle praise and little pick-me-ups when you're down always help.'
Harry, 18

Modern life can be incredibly stressful. Probably every generation that's ever existed and evolved have said this, but that doesn't make it any less true.

Today, the expectations of what family and personal life should be have been completely transformed from what they were, say, fifty years ago. In some ways this is a good thing. We undoubtedly have more freedom of choice and are less confined to traditional gender roles than we were in previous generations.

In terms of the smooth functioning of a family unit, however, some of the realities of contemporary culture have proved to be catastrophic. The introduction of gadgets and internet into the home mean that we are constantly stimulated and often don't have time to think and reflect. The increased consumption of convenience foods means our bodies are full of chemicals which make us juddery and irritable. The pressure to 'keep up with the Joneses' is stronger than it ever was and, what with the recent troubles in most of the economies around the globe, increasingly all parents within a family feel obliged to work full-time jobs.

As a direct result of these developments, many of us now feel that we are 'chasing time'. Whereas once the ability to fill our time with activities and homes with possessions were the currency of the day, in modern culture it is free time and space that we crave. We long for emptiness, silence and relaxation, and young people in particular are crying out for quality time and attention.

It's important at this juncture to note that, whilst I am about to describe some typical family situations which might have a negative impact on the self-esteem of children and young people, I am in no way placing blame. *The scenarios I'm about to list have been picked precisely because they are so common in today's society and the sort of things which are being experienced by people throughout the Western world. No family is textbook perfect and, even if it were, their shiny perfection would in itself cause problems and issues! We cannot control the challenges and misfortunes which come our way, we can only control how we deal with them. Later in the book, I will suggest ways in which effective communication can minimise damage to self-esteem in children. Below are some of the key life events which* *can be crossroads on life's journey, with each path representing a potential effect on self-esteem.*

CHILDHOOD

There is no way to measure self-esteem, however most psychologists would argue that people are born, if not with different amounts of it, with varying propensities for it. Whilst self-esteem is very much defined by the events of our life, it's entirely possible for two children to be brought up in exactly the same way, having identical experiences and emerge with different amounts of self-esteem.

It's also important to understand the distinction between being 'outgoing' and 'confident' or having self-esteem. Some children are naturally vocal, expressive and bubbly but they are still capable of suffering from a lack of self-esteem. Other children are naturally more reserved and quiet, yet this doesn't mean they can't have high self-esteem, if they are generally content with who they are.

Being naturally sensitive is a key defining element in self-esteem because sensitive people tend to over-analyse. Over-analysis quite often leads to feeling that situations are somehow our 'fault' even if we could not possibly have influenced them. It also means that outside negativity can be absorbed, internalised and endlessly re-hashed, leading to anxiety and other related issues.

Childhood is considered particularly important in establish-ing our self-esteem and family is often a potent force in its development. Parents and carers are leading by example, in this aspect. Much of the way in which we think and behave as children (laying down the blueprint for our behaviour in later life) is picked up subconsciously in our early years. This explains how we can disagree with the way our own parents spoke to us when we were young yet find ourselves repeating the exact same phrases to our own children, years later.

The most important action to take in ensuring your children will have high amounts of self-esteem is, therefore, first to work on your own. We receive our early personality and influences from those around us.

Whereas in young children self-esteem can quite literally be 'given', when adolescence is reached and children become more independent, they need to actively seek self-esteem if they wish to improve it. This is true of all adults. You cannot force someone to have high self-esteem, unfortunately. Having said that, your teenager will always continue to need a strong and secure relationship with their parent or carer so that they can meet the challenges they will face as they broaden the scope of their life.

FAMILY ENVIRONMENT

It is now relatively unusual for a child's parents to remain together as a couple for their entire lives, meaning that our understanding of a family unit has become much more complex. Step-parents, girlfriends and boyfriends and 'half'-siblings are now common fixtures in the modern family.

When two parents separate, it is not always necessarily a terrible thing for their children, as it is so often portrayed. Quite often, in fact, the child will find their parents' separation a welcome relief from the tension or fighting that preceded the split. It is better to have separated parents who are happy than those who are together and miserable.

What is essential is that divorce or separation are handled in the right way. The effect that separation can have on children, whether negative or positive, is pretty much always tangible, but so long as the people around them are vigilant and work together it can be supported positively.

If you are going through a separation, it will always be an incredibly difficult time for you. However, it is important that you allow your child to talk about their own feelings, entirely separate and irrespective of yours. Try not to influence them, but ask them open questions such as 'tell me how that makes you feel'. It's important that teenagers in particular do not feel that they are under interrogation at this stage. Younger children might also wish to express their feelings through drawing or play.

Try to resist the temptation to extract information about your estranged partner from your child. Questions such as 'what does Daddy's new girlfriend look like?' will instantly make your child feel as though they are a pawn in your games. Although incredibly difficult, try also not to say anything negative about your ex-partner in front of your child. Any bitterness or resentment is likely have a knock-on effect of making your child feel either confused or guilty.

Where possible, children must always be made to feel that their parents are still friends, with a united approach. This will also insure you to some degree against your child trying to play his or her parents off against each other. It's important that the path is cleared for the child to have a free relationship with each of their parents on their own terms, unencumbered by the feelings of their other parent(s).

In instances where parents are going through a disagreement, but are not intending to split up, again children should be shielded from this as much as possible. Wherever viable, arguments should happen out of a child's earshot. It's crucial that they are never made to feel like they have to take sides, or that they are being used as a confidante. Either of these scenarios will make them feel as though it is they who are parenting you. It's not always possible to prevent a child from hearing raised voices or picking up on tension, but in these cases they should always know that the disagreement is between the adults in the situation and has nothing to do with them. Children should also be reassured that the dispute is temporary and that their parents are working through something that will be resolved in the future.

WORK/LIFE BALANCE
In situations where parents are either together and both working, separated and working, or a single parent who has to work, this can create strain within the home. The work/ life balance which is essential to happiness will be thrown into disarray. Parents who have to work and run a home often feel stressed, tired, perhaps resentful at their lack of free time and generally as though their heads are full of urgent, unfinished tasks. This can cause a negative atmosphere and children are incredibly attuned and susceptible to atmosphere, often feeding off the mood that has been created by their parents.

Redundancy or unemployment can, sadly, have a similar negative impact on atmosphere, if a parent is constantly worrying about how they will pay the bills.

Wherever it is viable, children should always be shielded from money worries and it should not be discussed in front of them. Transferring money concerns onto children can be very damaging and is another way of instilling guilt. It's important to remember that the things you might perceive as financial hardships, your child might not even notice. Many adults say that they have a sudden realisation, once they are older, that they grew up in a 'poor' household. However, because they were happy, or were given a lot of time and attention, it simply did not register at the time. There are worse things than a child not having the latest pair of trainers.

BEREAVEMENT

Bereavement is another life event which can have a dramatic impact on children. Depending on the child's age, it can cause them to question everything about their life, raising big existential dilemmas about the afterlife.

Whatever the loss to a family, it will probably have a domino effect on everyone within it, which can make children feel as though they have lost a support network or have no one to talk to. In both of these cases, giving children the space and time to talk about what they are thinking and feeling is the key. Remember also not to get your own emotions of grief and loss mixed in with theirs and to let them have their own individual experience, with a right to feel however they do. However painful it might be to reminisce about the person you have lost or look at photographs so soon after the event, if that is what your child wants to do, it's important they know that you will allow them to do so. Young people often find pictures and keepsakes very comforting during this time.

NUTRITION

With so many demands on our time, cooking from scratch is fast becoming a thing of the past. After a long hard day, it's far easier to order a pizza or stick a ready meal in the microwave than to spend hours slaving over a hot stove. There's also the added pressure of nutritious food often being seen as more expensive (although this isn't always the case), as well as all the conflicting diet and health advice out there.

It is unusual now for a family to sit down together for dinner every night, owing to the demands on all of their time (vast amounts of homework from school not being the least of these). This takes away a source of potential stability, routine and quality time which was available to previous generations of children.

Eating poor quality food full of additives can also fuel a bad atmosphere in a house. High amounts of sugar, salt and chemicals can shorten our attention spans, make us more temperamental and make it harder for us to sleep.

There are simple, cost and time-effective ways to eat nutritious food (such as jacket potato and tuna or pasta in tomato sauce). For anything more complicated, forward planning and organisation will be needed – as a working mum, I know exactly how difficult this can be. The occasional ready meal or takeaway never harmed anyone, but it's also important to recognise the place food has within the family environment.

CONCLUSION

Low self-esteem is so often attributed to childhood experiences, the implication being that parents and carers are automatically and solely to blame. This is a harmful way to think, both for your own peace of mind and also because it usually isn't true.

Children are influenced by everything and everyone around them, a great deal of which is outside of a parent's control.

Whatever challenges you and your family face, children and young people can be helped towards having the resilience they need in order to emerge from those experience with their self-esteem intact. As long as they feel that their needs and emotions are both heard and valued and are, wherever possible, kept separate from the adult dramas happening around them, they can be sheltered from the worst aspects of family difficulties.

Whilst every parent will at some point wish they had spoken or acted differently, as long as there is a stable foundation whereby your child knows they are unconditionally loved and accepted, they have the building blocks they need to establish the self-esteem they require to equip them for life.

Simple acts, like leaving notes around for your child to find, perhaps on their mirror or underneath their pillow, reminding them that you are proud of them, will go a long way to boosting their confidence.

CHAPTER 4

THE LOW SELF-ESTEEM GENERATION

Natasha

It's really strange, being me. One day I'll be in a school chatting to a group of teenagers about cyber-bullying and the next day I'll be on Sky News, responding to news stories about the CYBER BULLYING EPIDEMIC that's sweeping the nation and invariably challenging the daft and sensationalist spins the press put on it.

Whilst, technically, I can't find anything to disagree with in the stats reported in the press it's fair to say that my on-the-ground experiences aren't as doom-y and gloom-y as the research might lead you to believe.

Yes, self-esteem issues are affecting a record number of young people, but that's only an ennui-inducing notion if you only see the problems, without context of them being housed within an actual person. Simply because someone is enduring something unpleasant does not entirely prohibit them from being wonderful, or from contributing meaningfully to society. Self-esteem issues might limit potential, but that is not the same as potential not existing in the first place.

So, whilst below I have set out my theories as to the causes and impacts of low self-esteem within a broad social context, it's important to always remember that there isn't a generation of middle-aged people throughout history who haven't to some extent laboured under the delusion that we're all going to hell in a handcart and teenagers are the ones guiding us into the flames. Reassuringly, they were always wrong.

The causes and impacts of low self-esteem are 'chicken and egg' in nature. So, for example, if a person is battling with a mental health issue it might prevent them from being able to hold down a job. Yet the very fact of widespread unemployment is a factor in the stresses and anxieties experienced by young people, thereby increasing the likelihood that they will become depressed.

Similarly, spending a huge amount of time on social media has been linked to a heightened compulsion to compare ourselves to others, which then bashes self-esteem because we cease to see ourselves as individuals but instead within a terrifyingly global pecking order. By the same token, people with low self-esteem are likely to seek refuge in social media, a sphere in which they are able to present an 'airbrushed' version of themselves for the delectation of online admirers. Confusingly, however, the solution would not be solely to spend less time on social media, since increased internet use is a cause of low self-esteem but also usually a symptom of a separate, unrelated cause.

Phew. See why we needed to write a whole book about this?

Anyway, here are some of the social contributors/results of low self-esteem of which I speak:

ECONOMICS

Sometimes, if I'm feeling particularly whimsical, I ring my mum and ask her to tell me the story about how, when she was a young lass, you could get a normal job and earn enough money to live your life. In late-seventies/early-eighties Essex, she assures me, basic wages would be sufficient for you to be able to afford a mortgage, maintenance of a vehicle and maybe even to go out to a 'disco' once a week. And though she is always careful to stress that you wouldn't necessarily be in a ten-bedroomed mansion with a Rolls Royce drinking Krug every Saturday evening (and that strict budgeting and a bit of self-restraint were usually necessary to get by) I still stare at the phone in wide-eyed wonder, imagining such a glorious, utopian era.

It seems incredible now, the idea that working class people might be able to afford to live in relative comfort, without pay day loans and overdrafts and constant hand-wringing when the time comes to pay the electricity bill. Owen Jones (a left-wing journalist) said in an article for the *Independent* (in which he rather brilliantly wrote the speech that the Leader of the Opposition should have given – but didn't – to win voters back around), that when we look back on this era in history the thing we will be most ashamed of is that only the relatively rich can really afford to live.

BLEAK. And bleaker still if you happen to be a teenager and thinking about your own economic prospects.

There are very few young people, even those who get jobs at the higher end of the starter scale, who can realistically afford to live completely independently. At some point in the past twenty years, wages went '*Sod it, I'm fed up of trying to keep up with inflation. I'm knackered*' and dropped out of the race. Long gone are the days where your parents booted you out at sixteen, declaring you now to be an adult who must fend for themselves and then had a party to celebrate their newly rediscovered liberty. It's now entirely normal to live with your folks in your twenties and thirties.

I was in London when the 'boomerang generation' thing happened. It was hideous. There we were, in our late twenties, on the cusp of 'proper careers', working like demons during the week before cracking open cheap bottles of wine and having parties on the crumbling rooftop terraces of our East London flats at the weekend. We bought our clothes from charity shops and called them 'vintage'. We walked everywhere. We blogged about how we were poor but happy. Then, one by one, our friends announced that they couldn't even afford to rent a room anymore. They went home to Wales, or the Midlands or 'up North' somewhere and had to face the terrible indignity of returning to suburbia after having been mocked for 'going up Town' to pursue their artsy-fartsy aspirations. But at least we got a small taste of the sort of life my Mum reminisces about (although none of us had cars). Our younger brothers and sisters couldn't even entertain the notion of flying the nest without considerable financial backing.

In your childhood home, you'll never feel older than twelve. You'll never truly discover who you are in such close physical proximity to all the things that remind you of being a child. Without independence we fester. And festering causes the object, in this case the self-esteem, to dissolve.

UNEMPLOYMENT

The employment market as it currently stands provides a rather discomforting presence in many young people's lives. At the time of writing, 817,000 British sixteen to twenty-four year olds are unemployed – approximately 18 per cent. Of those, 213,000 have been long-term unemployed (for more than one year)*. This figure did stand firmly at one million until recently, then miraculously dipped with the widespread use of 'zero hours contracts' (which are in my humble opinion the worst thing to happen to the working classes since Thatcher closed the mines).

Young people go through their school years being told that if they get a decent set of qualifications it will guarantee them a job. All employers seem to want, however, is experience. Quite often, they require extensive experience in the **precise** equivalent role that the candidate happens to be applying for. (So not the one week of 'work experience' they were forced to do just prior to taking their GSCEs, then).

By the time one gets to A Level, one is expected to do an average of four hours' homework a night. So that means that in order to have any chance of finding employment, one must find time in addition to those four hours to a) decide exactly what job one will apply for the second one is released from the clutches of the educational establishment and b) get in-depth experience of that specific role. Add into the mix the fact that even blue collar jobs are hugely oversubscribed (by a factor of up to 160 applicants for every position in some areas of the country, according to a report this year in the *Daily Mail*) and the entire situation makes you want to bang your head against the nearest solid object.

A huge chunk of our young people are, through no fault of their own, destined to be unemployed for their first few months or even years after leaving education.

Unemployment has a peculiar, cumulative effect on self-esteem. It's a bit like losing weight. In a logical world, someone who was, say, 30 stone and found it impossible to get out of bed would have more motivation and impetus to lose weight than someone who was 13 stone and couldn't fit into their size 12 jeans because they'd pigged-out on holiday. Yet we all know it doesn't work like that. It's like a vortex that sucks you in, and the further you are towards the bottom of the spiral the more momentous a task it is to claw your way out. In the same way, the longer you are unemployed the harder it is to get a job, both because of the holes in your CV and the dramatic effect unemployment has on the mind-set.

I have been unemployed for a total of one year during my adult life, over two periods, once directly prior to setting up my own business (a move I was advised against by Job Centre employees, as it was deemed 'too risky' – presumably more so than attempting to live on £35 a week unemployment benefit). Both times it was as though I could physically feel my sense of self-worth being sucked out of me. It's degrading, having to go and queue up to hold your hand out for a little bit of cash like some sort of Dickensian urchin. The outside world stops existing, to a degree – you sort of fold in on yourself. You know you can't afford **anything**, not even a cappuccino, so you stop looking around you and start to inhabit your own head, instead.

A key part of self-esteem is recognising how you fit into the world and your value within it. If you know without a shadow of a doubt that you aren't contributing to society, in fact you are actively taking from it, it makes you feel guilty for existing. That's even without the hundreds of rejection letters and emails you get each week which physically spell out your uselessness, because you're overqualified, or underqualified, or the position has been filled internally or through the nepotism they won't admit to.

Being unemployed chips away at your soul, a little bit every day, until you don't even recognise yourself anymore. It takes a rock-solid foundation of self-worth to endure that experience unscathed.

*Figures taken from Parliamentary document, House of Commons Online Library.

POLITICS

I should preface the following rant by saying I absolutely adore Russell Brand, when he's talking about how we should tackle drug addiction (during which he is magnificent) or his 'little winkie' and who he has put it in (during which he is hilarious). But the day he was interviewed by veteran political interrogator Jeremy Paxman and advised his (predominantly young) following not to vote because the establishment is broken, I hated him. I hated him with the passion of a thousand burning hot suns. I hated him using long words to sound clever and persuasive when he didn't appear to actually understand the meaning of them. I hated him for merely parroting the word 'revolution' in an increasingly maniacal fashion when asked what viable alternative there is to the 'broken' establishment. Most of all I hated him for deliberately exacerbating what is already a massive problem within our society.

At the time of writing, just 32 per cent of eighteen to twenty-four year olds voted in the most recent election and a recent Sky News poll revealed that a paltry 12 per cent intend to vote in the next one. They need absolutely no encouragement in the non-voting department. As a direct result, this particular demographic have been subjected to cuts to services equivalent to 28 per cent of their annual household income (many of which are to mental health services) under this government alone. Conversely, those aged fifty-five to seventy-four, who voted to the tune of 74 per cent at last count, had only 10 per cent of their services cut under austerity measures designed to combat the global recession.* And is it any wonder? What possible incentive could the people that govern us have for catering to the needs of citizens who won't vote either way? What's in it for them? Why should they bother?

Adding fuel to this kind of collective social apathy is dangerous because, until such time as there is the sort of 'revolution' Brand speaks about in the vaguest possible manner, young people are fated to enjoy the shitty end of the proverbial stick. Self-esteem isn't just about knowing you're a vital cog in the machinery of your environment, it's about knowing that, if necessary, you could directly impact and influence that environment.

I have never understood why Religious Studies is mandatory up until Year 9 in schools and yet political education is a tiny component of the 'Citizenship' curriculum, which is usually not taught by teachers with specialist knowledge in the subject. Studying religion gives students crucial information about how people think and behave differently according to their ideologies, but surely politics are just as powerful motivators in this regard? Allowing young people to understand how the fabric of our society is woven together, teaching them the difference between the political parties (historically and contemporaneously) and how their policies directly impact our country, our home towns and our lives should, surely, be given an equal amount of priority?

Whenever I ask about this apparent-anomaly, I'm told that teachers have a reputation for being left-leaning and it is therefore feared that they will unfairly influence their students towards socialism or a Labour vote if they are allowed to teach politics extensively. It's basically a 'section 28' style ruling (in which teachers were told they could not 'promote homosexuality' in the classroom) born out of fear and it is clearly hokum. If a Christian Religious Studies teacher can be trusted to remain neutral enough to teach children about Islam then a teacher who votes Labour should be able to talk about all the political parties in a similarly unbiased manner. It would be a start.

*Figures taken from a BBC report

ROLE MODELS

There is a school I visit which is in the centre of a council estate in East London. I'll never forget the first time I went there. It was 8 am and I saw some people doing a drug deal, in broad daylight. There were hoodies circling aimlessly on bikes. Imagine one of those kitchen-sink dramas British production companies make about the realities of the London 'hood' – I was in their opening scene.

When I arrived at the school, two of the Year 11s were smoking, in a really obvious way, right on the step outside the front door.

'*Er, WHO are you?*' one of them demanded.

'*Uhm, I'm teaching here today. If that's okay?*' I said. (At the time I had a fearful quaver in my voice but you can imagine I said this in a sarcastic manner if you'd like to imbue me with a retrospective coolness).

She just did that thing people do where they make their chin go right into their neck – a cross between an acknowledgment and surprise – which I took as my cue to go in.

As it turned out, I had a blast working with the Year 10 girls, who were, underneath all the bravado, fundamentally lovely. Yet I couldn't help but ask myself – if I lived here on this estate and went to this school what would my prospects be, realistically? What would I aspire to? Who would my role models be?

I was contemplating this as I bumped into a friend-of-a-friend in the school's reception. He worked in the financial district as some sort of banker-type-person and explained that he was there to take one of the Year 11 boys out for a coffee.

'To discuss what?' I asked, assuming it would be something specific.

'Stuff. Anything. Just to show him we're not so different.'

This struck me as being rather brilliant. The estate in question is shadowed by the immaculate, gleaming glass spires of the city's financial district. Men and women in suits who earn more money in one year than these children have seen during their entire lifetimes pass them every day, on their way to and from work. It's a perverse juxtaposition, really. You can just about see people moving around inside the gherkin from that estate. Two worlds – physically close – yet dramatically different.

I can imagine being a resident of that estate, seeing the 'hipsters' (wearing seven necklaces, silver trousers and a badger on their head) hanging out in the bars of neighbouring Shoreditch, or the bankers a little further down the road hastening along with their briefcases and their lattes in their hands and thinking they were entirely different species. Except of course they're not.

So this school had hit upon an ingenious plan: Let's get financial professionals to take our students for a hot beverage and a chat. It's not mentoring exactly and it's certainly not a particularly arduous commitment from either party. It's simply an effort to try and bring those two worlds closer together through communication and it's exactly the sort of thing young people need.

When people talk about 'role models' for the young, they'll usually then start speaking earnestly about pop stars and Hollywood actors and the terrible examples they set. When former squeaky clean Disney starlet Miley Cyrus released her music video for 'Wrecking Ball' (in which she cavorts, entirely starkers, on a gigantic, well, wrecking ball) the press went potty. They talked extensively about Miley's potential impact as a 'role model', yet you'll notice how few teenage girls there have been hanging around building sites naked since then. That's because, if you actually talk to teenage girls (as opposed to assuming that they are much stupider than you were when you were a teenager and **also** didn't mindlessly copy everything pop stars did) you'll discover that most of them thought that video was '*a bit weird*' and that Miley '*looked like a twat*'.

There is a difference between a role model and an idol. When I was thirteen I idolised Michael Jackson. I hero worshipped the guy. I wanted to know everything about him and his life. I watched endless documentaries about him (on VHS, I note, nostalgically). I copied all the dance moves from Thriller, because I had concluded they were cool. I would **not** have copied the dance moves from Thriller if Michael Jackson had been cavorting nude on industrial equipment instead (and I imagine the landscape of our collective musical history would have looked very different if he had been). I also did not start talking in an artificially high pitched voice or get a pet monkey. That's because I was a person in my own right with my own brain, as are the vast majority of young people in the world.

Having said that, there is, in my experience, a discrepancy between the way that girls and boys relate to pop culture icons. Young men are far more likely to directly emulate the behaviours, belief structures and ways of speaking of the people they idolise. I think this probably has less to do with the simple fact of their gender and is more an indicator of the relative lack of real-life male role models in a lot of boys' lives. As I type, two million households in the UK consist of one-parent families. Single mothers are still far more common than single fathers. Research at Nottingham Trent and Birmingham Universities has found that female teachers still dramatically outnumber men. So it's little wonder boys look for cultural role models and I think they'd be much less inclined to if they were shown examples of how to be a man closer to home.

Parents, older siblings, extended family, teachers, friends – these are young people's real role models, whether they like to think so or not. We glean far more from our immediate environment, by osmosis, than we do from anything else. Habits, language, political ideologies, attitudes, prejudices – these all inevitably come from the home, or, later, from our friendship groups.

Self-esteem comes from having a variety of role models in immediate proximity, showcasing diverse possibilities.

TECHNOLOGY

The other day I was describing an incident to an assembly of Year 10s which began with me being in the Southbank Centre in Waterloo 'people watching'. They all laughed, to which I said '*What?*' and one student replied '*So you just, like, WATCH people? That's really creepy, Miss.*'

(I then had to explain that people watching is actually an essential skill if you want to be a writer, at which point about half of them got their smart phones out to very earnestly make a note of that.)

What sort of world do we live in where observing real, three dimensional human interaction is considered 'creepy', yet invading someone's life by 'following' them on Twitter and proceeding to be privy to every random thought they have – the bus is slower than usual today and they really like pickled onion Monster Munch – is not?

Anyway, there's a whole chapter about the internet forthcoming so I shall stop there. Suffice to say we aren't going to reverse technological advancement. Social networking is here to stay. But its impact on young peoples' understanding of themselves and their environment is devastating, with (as far as I can see) very few redeeming counter points.

THE EDUCATION SYSTEM

There's a brilliantly inspiring TED talk called 'Schools Kill Creativity' by Sir Ken Robinson. If you have not seen it, I absolutely insist you do so immediately… On your smart phone which will conveniently allow you to do so instantaneously. (Okay, perhaps technology isn't ALL bad).

In his speech, Sir Ken speaks about how, if you followed

our education system through to its logical conclusion, you would become a university lecturer. That's pretty much as far as education in Britain can take you, professionally. So, he argues, we are essentially training young children from the age of four to become university lecturers. Our education system is one giant pyramid scheme.

The problem is, of course, that not every child either wants to be, or is cut out to be a university lecturer. So anyone with a skill set outside the strictly academic will fall by the wayside of our very linear curriculum. It's like being on a train to Lecturesville with stops at GSCE Town, A Level Avenue, Degree County and Masters Central, knowing at some point you'll be unceremoniously booted off because you can't understand what your fellow passengers are talking about any more.

The responsibility for whether or not your unique talents are a) recognised and b) nurtured within the school environment therefore falls almost entirely at the discretion of your individual teachers. These are the same teachers whose professional worth is judged solely on the grades their students get in exams which are designed to measure one tiny corner of the huge spectrum of human skill.

So-called 'vocational' qualifications are still looked upon rather sneerily as the sort of thing you do if you're not 'bright' enough to do anything else, an idea solidified by the present government, who cut huge swathes of them.

It's infuriating in a way that even I can understand, and I am someone who was always interested in learning purely for learning's sake and kept my cool in exams, thus making me the ideal candidate for sailing through the system as it stands (but not, interestingly, for automatically getting a job at the end of it – see 'unemployment' above). I have friends who are talented in ways I really can't fathom – like construction (I can't even assemble Ikea furniture), mechanics (when my driving instructor asked me '*What would you do if your car broke down on the motorway?*' I said '*Call my Dad!*'), sport and arts – whose self-esteem was squished almost to non-existence simply by having to go into school every day and being rubbish at everything that happened within its walls.

It breaks my heart when people tell me that they are '*stupid*'. I hear it all the time, and not just from teenagers. It's such a self-limiting way to label yourself and it usually stems from experiences at school. The people who have been made to feel this way often blame their teachers, but I think we must acknowledge that, the majority of the time, teachers have their hands tied by the system and find the situation as frustrating as everyone else.

As a wonderful teacher I worked with recently called Mary Meredith sagely said '*The syllabus would be great preparation for life, if life was a pub quiz.*'

Add to that the fact that, despite successive governments and their constant 'reforms' of the education system, and the constant parade of new strategies and curriculum changes that have driven teachers to distraction, the structure of the education system, at its core, has barely been updated for the past fifty years. The only solution is, clearly, to completely start again from scratch, devising an education structure that allows everyone to fulfil their potential. This will require almost unthinkable, multiple-headache-inducing quantities of paperwork, people hours and generalised stress. Which is probably why they haven't done it.

CONCLUSION

Please don't mistake me, the moral to be taken from this chapter is not that the situation is hopeless or that the low self-esteem epidemic amongst our youth was always, and continues to be, inevitable. Rather it was to illustrate my frustration that conversations surrounding mental health and self-esteem in teenagers only ever seem to scratch the surface.

Particularly within media reporting, there seems to be a constant urge to point the finger of accusation at one easily-identifiable root cause, when the truth is that our culture provides the fertile soil for low self-esteem to flourish, owing to a complex web of political and sociological factors. Social media, Photoshop and incessant celebrity worship are undoubtedly watering that soil, but the solid earth is composed of the sorts of things I've described above – things which are less easily analysed and dismissed.

A lot of my time is spent attempting to convince the powers-that-be that it's all very well us having a Parliamentary round table meeting specifically about body image, for example, but body image issues are a manifestation of a much wider and more complicated problem. If we really want to help young people there needs to be more of a unified approach. Without wishing to sound too much like a hippy, we need to work towards a better and fairer society for all – at which point a lot of the mental and physical health problems young people (and indeed all people) battle with will dissipate, or at least be easier to manage, as a consequence.

In the meantime, we can strengthen young people's mind-set, improve communication and nurture resilience. None of this is insurmountable with the right support and guidance.

(I think so anyway.)

CHAPTER 5

THE INTERNET/ TECHNOLOGY

Lynn

MONITORING AND ESTABLISHING BOUNDARIES WITH THE INTERNET AND TECHNOLOGY

The internet can be a wonderful, educational tool and children are often expected to use it as part of their schooling and homework. However, the online world can and does have a very dark side to it. As soon as your child logs onto the internet, in effect they open themselves up to everyone and everything, both good and bad, on the planet.

'Looking back, social networking had a negative influence on me, often deluding me into thinking everyone else was having more fun than me. This left me feeling that I was inadequate and that made me feel lonely.' *Joe, 25*

It is expected that we generally know where our kids are, who they are with or what they are doing at any given time of the day. Yet in the digital world, where even our youngest children are increasingly spending a lot of their time, we as parents are reduced to spectators. Many of us are left reeling from a case of 'digital whiplash' – our children may well understand technology better than we do.

Kids today have only known a world that is cyber-filled and technology has influenced every aspect of their lives. It informs their friendships, their education, their leisure time and even their growing understanding of the world. Meanwhile, we are left trying to figure out which rules we should set and how we should enforce them.

'Social networking is actually making our children antisocial. When they are with their friends, instead of looking them in the eye and laughing, they have one eye on their phone, checking what they are missing.'
Marie, mother.

There is a designated age when we can drink, smoke and have sex. The internet has just as much impact on our lives as any of these things and yet there are no official guidelines on the right time to venture into cyberspace. Online life tends to start at an early age and accelerate very quickly. There are the Disney interactive games, Nintendo DS, the Wii and before they know it children venture onto YouTube, where they find a treasure-trove of information and stimulation, both positive and negative. The 'right' age for a child to log onto the internet varies for each individual. Ideally, each website would be rated for age-appropriate content, but because of the instant, snowballing nature of the internet this is unfortunately very unlikely to happen.

My parents used to overhear my childhood phone conversations on the landline. Our only phone was kept in the hall of our house. Now, so much communication goes on silently out of our range and knowledge, over text, social networking and via mobile phones.

Preventing your child from using the internet or a mobile phone won't keep them safe, so the only way forward is to allow them to undertake these activities under guidelines and supervision. As ever, communication is the key to getting this one right. Introducing conversations around technology should ideally happen as soon as children are able to speak. It's important that they know they can talk to you about it.

GAMING SYSTEMS

By nursery age (three and four years old) many kids can nimbly work the controls of an X-Box, Nintendo or online computer game.

Never assume that any game is age appropriate unless you have checked it out yourself. Put off any network games (which allow communication and interaction with other gamers) until your child fully understands online safety.

As your child begins gaming, monitor their behaviour and the way that they talk. This will let you know how much time they should be spending on the game. If it begins to affect their attention span or mood, then they have spent too long on the game.

Set a limit for how long your child should spend playing

computer games each week. Be wary of the 'But I've got to finish this level or I'll lose everything I've done!' excuse. Once or twice is okay, any more than that and they have found a way to extend the weekly time limit.

Be aware of how close your child is sitting to the screen. If they are consistently sitting very close, they may have problems with their vision and should see an optician.

MOBILE PHONES

By Year 5 of school (age nine and ten) your child will probably have friends who carry mobile phones.

At the age of ten your child most likely does not need a mobile phone, but by eleven or twelve they will be becoming more independent. Probably the right age for your child to have a mobile will be whenever they are spending time in situations where they might have to let you know where they are and if they have an emergency, e.g. shopping with friends. Text messaging, WhatsApp and BBM are probably a huge component of your child's social world by secondary school age (eleven years) and many parents feel it is not fair to exclude them from this.

When you decide it is time, research your child's school's policy on possession and use of mobile phones on the premises.

Many mobile phone providers allow you to limit the numbers that can be dialled and received, as well as text messaging and web downloads, and it is worth checking this out. You will find that most phone shops are happy to talk you through these options, as well as the phone's settings, if you are unsure.

Most phones can now take photos and videos, meaning that your child can potentially put themselves at risk without fully understanding what they are doing. It's vital to talk frankly with your child about what not to shoot or send and for them to be aware that, once something is posted on the internet it creates an indelible cyber record which can never be truly deleted. It is worth pointing out at this stage that this is also the case with the popular app 'Snapchat'. This allows people to send pictures to each other which are then 'deleted' automatically after a few seconds when reaching the receivers' device. Many young people (wrongly) think this is a way to send information with no consequences. Apart from anything else, there is nothing stopping the receiver taking a 'screenshot' of the picture which would then give them a permanent record of it.

EMAIL

Again, this is something children are keen to access from around the age of eight. To begin with, you might want to give your child access to a family account which they can use to communicate with their friends from time to time. By eleven or twelve they might wish to have their own email, but it would be shrewd to explain to them that you will check their inbox regularly to ensure that they are behaving appropriately and that their friends are not stepping over the line in terms of tone and content.

You should be open about how and when you intend to conduct monitoring of online accounts, so that you cannot be accused of 'snooping'.

INTERNET

Children of Junior level (eight and above) need access to the internet in order to do their homework assignments. Most web providers allow you to set parental controls, allowing you to block certain websites that may have adult or inappropriate content. As your child grows older, you can loosen the controls gradually.

It's easier to have conversations about online safety little and often, rather than trying to cover everything all at once, which confuses everyone involved. As your children get older and technology advances and changes, make sure that you continue talking about what they are doing online and that you, to the best of your ability, keep abreast of these changes.

To understand exactly what your children are doing online, try asking them about their favourite website, why they enjoy it and what their favourite features are. Try to keep the chat light and casual, rather than accusing. This will keep you one step ahead of them. Let your children show you how to use websites and games. Children and young people often enjoy showing their parents what they have learned and achieved and this is a way for you to use their potentially superior technical knowledge to your advantage. It also means you are showing them support, which they will appreciate.

There are conversational ways to approach any subjects you might be worried about, in terms of cyber safety. Ask your teenagers what tips they would give to other teens who wanted to protect themselves online. When they volunteer what they know, ask them how they learned that. Ask your child to help you set up a profile on social media – this way you can check to see whether they know about privacy settings (which determine how much of the information they display can be seen by the general public) and whether they are likely to have applied these to their own accounts.

You could play a game with your child online. This will give you an insight into the game, whether it is appropriate for their age and how they are interacting with others on the internet.

In terms of setting time limits, owing to the clandestine nature of the internet (sometimes you don't know if they are on a website or reading a book on their Kindle, for example, since from the outside the two activities appear exactly the same), some parents find it helpful simply to turn the router off at a certain time of day, to provide a definite 'cut off point'.

ONLINE 'FRIENDS'

'Social networking is a double edged sword – it is a means by which my daughter can keep up with her friends, yet it has highlighted the gulf between their world and hers.'
Jennifer, mother.

Today's young people don't think of those they have met online through social networking and gaming as strangers, they class them as friends. It's important to try and ascertain who they are talking to and how choosy they are being about who they befriend online.

Ask them who has the most online friends out of everyone they know. You could try asking them how it is possible to have so many friends. It's crucial to explain that people are capable of lying about their personal details – age, gender and photograph – online and encourage your child to have a healthy degree of suspicion towards anyone they talk to on the web.

Try accessing your child's social networking accounts from outside, whilst not logged into the website, to ascertain just how much sensitive information they are giving away.

Probably the biggest danger to young people on the web is that they will be sucked into an online 'community' who engage in dangerous practices, such as self-harm or anorexia as a 'lifestyle'. The web links us to other like-minded people, so that behaviours which aren't normal become normalised. Again, monitoring and communication will help you to assess whether or not your child might have become sucked into a potentially dangerous online forum, as will the language that they use. If they suddenly begin using slang terminology relating to eating disorders or self-harm, then it is likely that they learned these by talking to others online.

As everybody uses social networks, it is all too easy to sometimes get caught up in what other people are doing, comparing yourselves to them. Events can often be exaggerated and this distorts reality, causing us to worry and review our lives.' *Kim, 21*

CONCLUSION
The internet is one of those things which, as a parent, can make you feel as though you are losing control over your children. With communication, guidelines and boundaries, that control can be regained in a way that does not feel intrusive to your child.

ARTICLE: WAKE UP – TWITTER IS REAL LIFE
By Natasha Devon

First published in *Cosmopolitan* magazine, April 2014

Asking someone how much they love the prospect of social networking is like chopping down a tree and counting the rings

– an easy way to determine age, with an accuracy factor of up to seven years.

My mum simply cannot fathom why anyone would want to post mundane details about their private life onto public forums (or why anyone else would look at them). Teenagers, conversely, inhabit a world defined by cyber-happenings. Professor Rachel Thompson, who is currently studying the effects of 'digital childhoods', has concluded that for teenagers now, school and family time are in fact mere 'pauses' in their social, online existences. Real, human interaction is fast becoming a minor irritation to be endured between Instagram-ing.

I languish somewhere in the middle ground. Social media doesn't dominate my day, yet my phone is the first thing I reach for in the morning (because it's my alarm clock). I cannot resist that first opportunity to have a sneaky glance at email, Twitter etc., in case some massive event of global significance has occurred whilst I was asleep. (That's my excuse, anyway!)

Earlier this year, Caroline Criado-Perez, a feminist campaigner, successfully took the blusteringly indignant morons who threatened her and her family with rape and murder on Twitter to court. (She had dared to suggest that Jane Austen should be the new face on our ten pound notes. I know... Outrageous!) The two worst offenders were recently sentenced to jail terms, with the judge saying their threats had caused Caroline 'panic, fear and horror'. Their defence, bizarrely, was that they were bored.

The realisation that your online activities can now land you in jail provoked a backlash from some, claiming the cyber world is not 'real'. If we do not like what we see on social networks we can, they huffed, simply delete our accounts. Furthermore, if we imprison anyone who has ever said anything ill-advised on Twitter, huge swathes of the population will be sent down and our prisons are already stretched to capacity. All in all, they concluded, Caroline is just another goddamn attention-seeking feminist getting her proverbial knickers in a twist.

There are several reasons why this is daft. For one, the online sphere clearly is 'real' for most of us. A study at the end of last year revealed that 54 per cent of twenty-five to forty year old women would rather give up sex for a month than their smart phones. If that doesn't spell out our digital dependence, I don't know what does.

More importantly, harassment is in the eye of the beholder. Whilst the tweeter might get their jollies from haranguing a faceless victim, they can't know what state of mind the recipient will be in. The tragic example of Tallulah Wilson, the talented teenage ballerina who was driven to suicide in January by what she encountered on websites, is a poignant example of this.

What will and will not be tolerated online needs to be a) established and b) enforced. Fast. And we, as the generation able to take a balanced view from both sides of the technical revolution, might just be the gals to do it.

Natasha

THE GENERATIONAL DIVIDE

My partner Marcus is almost ten years older than me and thus a fully-fledged member of a generation that simply cannot fathom the impact of social media. He is on Facebook, of course, and Twitter, as is now prerequisite if you wish to be a member of the human race. But he is also prone to, I'd estimate, bi-daily rants on how the youth of today are veritably obsessed with their smart phones and this fact heralds the disintegration of society as we know it. Luckily, I find ranting quite sexy.

Marcus' stance is a familiar one, because I hear similar sentiments expressed constantly from teachers and parents. The existence of the generation-based technological divide is not actually because it's outside the realms of an older adults' capability to understand the technology young people are using. Of course they could grasp the basic functions if they were explained to them. A trained baboon could probably glean the rudiments of Instagram.

The issue is the fact that 'grown ups' will never fully understand why the online world matters so much to people younger than them. In this regard, we can only ever sympathise, never empathise. We were not born into a culture where internet was instant and universally accessible. We cannot comprehend the extent to which the young become immersed in the net and surrender themselves to it. We are likely to baulk at the idea that, for them, social networking is not a hobby but a way of life.

Grace Dent, *Independent* columnist and one of my heroes, argues in her book *How to Leave Twitter* that online 'friends' are in some ways more meaningful than the ones you make in the real world. That's because your connection with online friends is based purely on shared interests or humour, rather than the simple fact of having come from the same town, or working in the same building. She's right, of course. Grace Dent is always right. But I'd still hesitate to instant message a mate off Facebook if, say, I went into labour suddenly and needed a lift to hospital, rather than picking from amongst my friends in the world of three dimensions. That is because I am in my thirties and therefore have a generationally dictated emotional distance from cyber space.

Once, a much younger woman who follows me on Twitter direct messaged me to tell me she had taken an overdose. After freaking out because I didn't have her address, phone number, location or any of the other required information to deal with the situation (and eventually persuading her that she MUST tell her mum in 140 character chunks of text) I contemplated what a strange thing that was to do.

Clearly, young people do **not** have emotional distance from the cyber sphere. For them, the internet is indistinguishable from what we might call 'the real world'.

There is little point in simply ridiculing young people for this because we cannot understand it. Instead, it is far more helpful to reflect upon where the desire to spend so much time online comes from, what they are exposed to on the web and, most importantly, what collective emotional needs are being highlighted by their online behaviours. We can then answer the crucial question: what is it that we, as the adults in their life, are not providing them with that the internet, apparently, can?

SOCIAL MEDIA

Every time I host a workshop, I ask students to raise their hands to indicate whether they have membership to various social networks. I can therefore tell you that, at the moment, by far the most popular social networking sites amongst British teenagers are Instagram and Twitter.

This is very telling. Instagram is a website which allows you to post a series of pictures on your profile (with captions if desired), inviting other users to 'like' and comment on them. Twitter invites users to express themselves in a series of statements of no more than 140 characters, as well as to post photographs. It is clear from their relative popularity compared with social media sites which permit one to be more verbose that young people are becoming increasingly visual, as well as prone to thinking in terms of absolutes.

The rising prominence of the 'selfie' (a photograph taken of yourself then posted to social media) is often derided and mocked in the press and yet it does reflect something quite serious and, ironically, ugly, about the society in which we live. I should mention here that I am not a stranger to the selfie and I do understand the mentality behind them. My own selfies most often depict me in close proximity to interesting things. '*Look! Here I am next to an international sportsperson! Or a tortoise! Or the Leaning Tower of Pisa!*' Apparently, I feel an urgent need to document and share my experience of having been near certain people, objects and landmarks.

Journalists and experts have hypothesised that my particular style of selfie is indicative of a latent belief that if I am not able to prove empirically, or more specifically visually, that something happened, it did not happen at all. I think it is more likely just a bit of good, old fashioned, relatively harmless showing-off.

I am concerned, however, when I see Instagram accounts which consist pretty-much solely of completely context-less selfies. Many users don't even bother to pretend that they are showcasing a new outfit, or hairstyle. It is simply a case of '*I am raising awareness of my own face*'. Applying the 'visual evidence' theory above, I can only assume that people who consistently post pictures of this nature are labouring under the delusion that they do not exist. Whatever happened to 'Cogito ergo sum'? If Descartes had lived today he probably would have written '*I selfie, therefore I am*' instead.

There are so many human traits that the selfie cannot capture. On even the most superficial physical level our attractiveness is inextricably tied up with qualities such as how we move, walk, speak and smell and how much we smile. The selfie renders itself pretty futile in capturing the essence of a person.

Yet if, by spending increasing amounts of time on websites like Instagram which bombard the user with imagery, young people come to value aesthetics above all else, is it any wonder many of them consider their physical appearance more important than their character?

Twitter, in the opinion of this self-confessed Twitter obsessive, is the most viciously addictive and potentially self-destructive popular social media site in existence. Grace Dent wrote a fantastically insightful article recently called 'Twitter is Stealing Your Life', in which she listed all the various ways in which a compulsion towards persistent Twitter use robs us of our time, energy and potential. She shared the link on Twitter and I read it because I was scrolling through my Twitter feed. After reading and agreeing with every word I retweeted the article and then went back to looking at Twitter. Like so many emotion-based urges, my desire to spend time on Twitter was not diminished by the knowledge that it was bad for me.

Twitter's greatest cruelty is that it robs the user of the ability to use subtlety and nuance. When one's opinion must be expressed in 140 characters or less, one will sound as though one is shouting ALL THE TIME. You know when politicians start to waffle on Question Time because they can see both sides of an argument and David Dimbleby keeps saying 'Yes or no? Yes or no?' in their ear hole until they look like they might cry? Twitter is the universal Dimbleby to our floundering MP.

The culture of Twitter is aggressive for that very reason and it isn't a forum I would recommend for anyone vulnerable.

Whether it's Twitter or Instagram, unless you apply specific security settings to your account, other users do not have to ask your permission to follow you (applying these settings immediately disables the ability to use other, quite groovy functions on the site, which is why people don't tend to do it). When we establish a profile on these sites we open ourselves up to the world and its judgement. Millions of strangers, with all their issues and prejudices, have direct access to our phones.

When you are growing up, you probably haven't experienced even one thousandth of the massive spectrum of Human Fuck-up-ery. You do not yet understand that other people's assessments of you are usually a reflection of their own state of mind. You cannot comprehend the compulsion some people have to be deliberately hurtful, or to make the world agree with them. The worst thing you could possibly do, then, is create an online version of yourself and declare to the universe 'Hi! Here I am! This is me! Judge away!' Nothing will prepare you for what will inevitably follow.

Both the best and worst thing about social media is that it unites people who have similar opinions and interests. In a best case scenario, a teenager who feels isolated because they don't feel they can identify with anyone in their peer group will find solace online, where they will be united with a group of like-minded individuals. At worst, they will be relentlessly battered and bullied by a group of people whose ideology doesn't match their own and whose sense of moral superiority has been inflated by the fact that the online world has united them with people who agree with them.

The effect of social media on teenagers in particular is one of the few instances when, I believe, the press have not been unnecessarily hyperbolic. It would be hard to overestimate its impact. In fact, there has been some fascinating research done in the field of neuroscience, which has been able to show that spending huge amounts of time on social networking sites is actually changing the way young brains develop.

One example of this is that the part of the brain associated with comparing oneself to others (and being concerned with how we measure up as a consequence) has become enlarged. (I think that bit of the brain is at the front, just behind the forehead, but don't quote me on that because I'm not a neuroscientist). The effect of social networking sites is then magnified because whilst, on the one hand, a world of constant selfies, updates on our social whereabouts and generalised boasting creates a 'keeping up with the Joneses' type mentality, for those who have spent a lot of time on the internet during their formative years their brain has become predisposed to that way of thinking in the first place.

When asked to define self-esteem for a 2012 inter-school survey, Year 9 and 10 girls tended to say a variation on '*knowing we have a unique set of skills and talents and having those recognised*'. In the global community created by the internet, this is virtually impossible. There will always be someone better looking, cleverer and more talented than you are and the web gives you instant access to those people. As isolating as it might seem at the time, being aware of the things that make us different from the crowd is an essential building block in developing self-esteem.

As far as I can see, young people seek out social media because they crave attention, praise and stimulation. As a result, however, they may become overstimulated, develop narcissistic tendencies and eventually an inability to process and form their own opinions on what they see. It is our job to correct that.

Craving of Attention

It is important to regularly remind young people that they are valued, in the correct way. Later, in the Body Image chapter, I suggest ways to effectively praise children and young people for qualities that have nothing to do with **what** they are and everything to do with **who** they are.

When people with high self-esteem are surrounded by friends and family the resulting feeling of being unconditionally accepted and loved releases a chemical in the brain, responsible for a feeling of relaxation and contentment. People with low self-esteem block that chemical and so never feel that they are unconditionally accepted, at a primal level. If social media is eroding self-esteem, it stands to reason that young people need to be physically told and shown that they are unconditionally loved. There are a thousand ways to tell someone that they are special which have nothing to do with how they look or the grades they receive.

Overstimulation

Limiting time spent on social media can combat this somewhat, as can being very clear with children from their first foray into social media that there are millions of people online and most of them don't have a Scooby what they're talking about.

No Time for Reflection

Increased time spent on social media creates the sense of a 24 hour, fast paced world. Vicky Beeching, who is a theologian and social commentator, has spoken about how the constant stimulation provided by social media can actually induce feelings of guilt when we are simply 'doing nothing'.

'Doing nothing' is, however, essential for the human mind. Slowing down, relaxing and giving ourselves time to reflect allows us to process and to learn from the events of the day. Parents can lead by example in this regard. Show your children that you take time to relax and emphasise how important that is.

Parents and teachers can also help by asking young people open questions which will force them to analyse and process what they have seen online. Ask them things like *'What do you think about that?'* or *'Do you think he was right to say that?'* so that they aren't taking everything at face value.

Sometimes, in class, I show students a quick-tempo, hyper-visual online video and simply ask them *'What did you see, just then?'* It's a fantastic exercise because, of course, different students will have latched on to different aspects of the video, which can then give way to a debate about what the film was 'about'.

ONLINE BULLYING

Having been the target of online bullies (or 'trolls') I can say with some authority that it is a degrading and generally hideous experience. There is a disconnect between what one knows to be true, i.e. that the opinions of these people don't really matter, and what one feels, which is that somehow their opinion must be valid.

In terms of minimising emotional damage, I have found encouraging students to understand what motivates online bullies to be a useful exercise. After all, if I am happy, I will not feel the need to troll other people online in order to get my jollies. Sympathy for the bully diminishes their power.

In terms of response, there are two schools of thought. School one maintains that online bullies should never be given the oxygen of attention and therefore should be immediately blocked and ignored. School two believes that there is a moral obligation to 'name and shame' online bullies for their behaviour.

I tend to ally myself with the former camp. It's not always practically possible to 'shame' an online bully – they usually hide behind fake names and avatars. Even if they do not, they are quite often convinced that there is nothing wrong with their behaviour.

More often than not, trolling (just like any other form of bullying) is motived by the desire to 'get a rise' out of the target. Responding to the bully will not only prolong interaction, it will give the bully satisfaction in knowing they have provoked a reaction.

For cruel comments regarding appearance or opinions, I recommend blocking and then being very disciplined in not looking at what the perpetrator will continue to write about you online. That is the best way I found to deal with my particular situation, in terms of both extinguishing the bully's behaviour and minimising damage to my own self-esteem.

However, in cases where the victim feels that their safety might be at risk, it's important that they know they are entitled to tell the police. Victims of cyber bullying often feel that they will be laughed at by authority figures if they report online behaviours. This is not the case and police are obligated to take the complaint seriously and investigate if necessary.

INTERVIEW WITH KELLY YOUNG, EDUCATOR IN ONLINE PORNOGRAPHY

Natasha

Once, during some teacher training I was delivering, I happened to mention a fantastic resource I had stumbled upon (through the judicious use of Twitter) called 'Make Love Not Porn'. The website, created by entrepreneur and impressive force for social change Cindy Gallop, works on the basis that young people need to see a range of 'real' bodies engaging in more realistic sexual acts than the ones they are bombarded with on more mainstream pornography sites. To me, this is basic common sense. It's ridiculous to expect that teenagers will not go looking for pornographic material in the internet age – their natural curiosity coupled with their relative lack of actual bedroom experience virtually demands it.

About half of the teachers present turned bright red, began coughing nervously or laughing hysterically, such was their embarrassment at my even mentioning the topic of porn. One even shouted '*I don't think so!*' from the audience.

When you consider that Jameela Jamal's 2014 BBC3 documentary '*Porn: What's the Harm?*' revealed that 60 per cent of children are exposed to hard core pornography before the age of fourteen, it is clear that someone needs to step in to minimise the potential damage this might cause.

A survey undertaken by Young Minds revealed that four out

of ten young people believe that online porn has affected their ability to form relationships, whether romances or friendships. Journalist Martin Daubney's Channel 4 documentary *'Porn on the Brain'* examined the increasingly common addiction to online videos with extreme sexual content amongst young men. Research undertaken for the documentary by the University of East London showed that by the time they reached the age of sixteen a staggering 97 per cent of children had consumed porn on the internet. The girls surveyed in particular reported being distressed and even traumatised by what they saw. Later, Daubney described porn as *'the most pernicious threat facing children today'*.

Teachers often claim pornography is a topic which should be broached by parents in the home. I completely understand why they say this. It must be incredibly frustrating if you are, say, a maths teacher and form tutor, to suddenly be expected to address a highly sensitive and potentially embarrassing topic such as this with your class and then return to normal the following day. In an ideal world, of course this would be the remit of parents. However we must bear in mind that, however good we consider our relationship with our parents to be, the chances are we will find discussing masturbation aids with them excruciating.

As I am **constantly** saying when TV presenters try and pass the buck on PSHE subjects from schools to parents, we can't control what goes on behind the closed doors of every British home, but we can control what is taught in schools. If teachers for whatever reason feel they do not have the confidence or expertise to address such an important issue then, clearly, third parties need to be bought into the school environment.

DA DAAA! Enter Kelly Young, stage left – a rather brilliant woman who goes into schools to conduct pornography workshops. Hers is a fairly new discipline, not traditionally covered within broader sexual education. She is therefore one of only a handful of experts on what can be a veritable minefield. Here, I pick her brain:

Q: How widespread would you say exposure to hardcore porn is amongst young people?

It's not unusual at all for twelve year olds to have seen hardcore online pornography. In an average Year 8 group, around 50 per cent will say they have seen porn and those are just the ones that will actually admit to it.

We have to bear in mind that all this stuff is just a click away and virtually impossible to shield kids from. There was one primary school pupil I spoke to who said a boy in her class had asked her to type 'bald pussy' into Google because it would take her to a website where cats got shaved. So that was the first time she saw porn. That's quite often the kind of thing that leads to children being exposed to it and unless we explain it they won't understand what they are seeing.

In my experience, most adults simply don't realise the volume and content of the stuff that is out there.

I always advise parents not to let children have IT in their bedrooms but they're still always going to have their phones on them so it's not going to entirely protect them. There is only so much pornographic material that a firewall will catch, too. You can only restrict so much. The people who make these sites find sneaky ways of getting them out there.

Q: What frustrates you the most in the job that you do?

It has to be the number of schools that put limits on what I can say in a classroom environment. They don't understand that, whatever I say, the children have seen and heard a lot worse and by limiting me it limits the effectiveness of the work that I do. We need to talk about pornography openly. A lot of parents don't even know where to start and most teachers don't understand exactly how explicit the material out there is. Parents and teachers need assistance in dealing with the situation. I just wish that I had free rein to address the topics in the right way.

Q: What do you think would be the most helpful thing the powers that be could do to limit children's exposure to porn?

The government are going to put 'opt in' settings onto websites with explicit content (at the moment you have to opt out) but I'm not sure how much actual good that will do. If the email providers, like Hotmail and Google could limit spam mail that would be incredibly helpful. Sometimes the wording of spam emails can seem fairly innocent but the links contained within them are actually to porn sites.

Having said that, it's a massive undertaking for any internet provider to try and limit access. It would take a huge amount of expertise, people hours and money. Technology is being updated every day so whatever you put in place to block pornographic material someone is going to find a way to bypass it and the whole cycle begins again.

Q: What would you say was the impact of watching pornography on young people's lives?

There's this strange juxtaposition now of young people being incredibly sexualised at a young age but really very naive and immature at the same time. This is particularly true of boys.

When I undertake workshops with groups of boys I ask them what they have seen on the web and they immediately start throwing out all the slang terms they know for incredibly explicit sexual acts. They're also obsessed with anal sex. They have no problem talking about these things with me.

But when it gets down to it, they're not really mature enough to understand the meaning of what they're saying. They're keen to show off about the different terms and sexual acts they know, but their knowledge of basic things, like the human anatomy, is pretty pitiful. Once I was working with a Year 9 class labelling the different parts of the human body on a man and a woman and one of the boys asked me what a scrotum was. I told him he should know as he has one. Just minutes before he'd been talking about sex in really hardcore terms so it was unbelievable that he didn't know the correct term for his ball sack! They also tend to be really uncomfortable talking about emotions, so there's a whole side of sex that they don't understand.

For both girls and boys, porn informs their expectations of how real sex should be. For boys, they think that how the men act in these films is showing them how to be masculine. For girls they think this is how they should have to behave in order to be desired and wanted. There's absolutely nothing about a woman's pleasure in these videos. So they often put their own sexuality to one side and think it's all about pleasing the man.

It affects them outside the bedroom, too. The language that they use when they speak to each other is often quite bullying sexual langue, like calling girls 'sluts'. There's also a pecking order in peer groups based on who is the hottest girl and this will encourages them to behave in an overtly sexual way in order to be perceived as 'the hot one'. There's a status associated with having done certain sexual acts, and that is true within both male and female peer groups, but really it's about having someone who wants them. They often can't distinguish being fancied from being popular.

Q: What can schools do?

Staff can challenge bullying that uses sexual language. There is so much of it that goes on and if it was racist or homophobic it would probably be picked up on. I think teachers worry that they'd be sanctioning kids all day for it, but if the message is given that it isn't acceptable that would reduce the use of these terms. We need to think about what we are creating – this is a generation of kids who will probably end up calling each other sluts and whores in the work place if we don't tell them that it is unacceptable.

Sex education also needs to be updated and improved. Sex education still revolves about how a baby is made, STIs and periods. We have to bring in both the emotional aspects of sex (relationships) and pornography. Children know more about sex now at eleven than we did at twenty and they're well versed in the basic mechanics. They don't need to be told about what goes where.

If we carry on just telling them how to put a condom on and nothing else they're not going to connect that with their lives. They will end up feeling confused and lost.

*We also need to make PSHE mandatory for **everyone**. Muslim children are often pulled out of PSHE lessons and that means the girls don't get the vital information they need on things like female genital mutilation. The way it stands at the moment Catholic and Church of England schools are also allowed to opt out of sex education, but that means their children could end up being abused and not know how to stop it.*

Schools could also help by continuing the themes of PSHE in all lessons, so that the messages given are regularly reinforced.

CHAPTER 6

HOW TO CREATE A HIGH SELF-ESTEEM ENVIRONMENT

Lynn

CREATING A HIGH SELF-ESTEEM ENVIRONMENT AT HOME

A lot of the time, people seem to just expect children to have a healthy self-esteem. In reality, the need to create a high self-esteem environment should be acknowledged from day one and instilling self-esteem will require constant effort.

As stated already, self-esteem, positivity and confidence tends to filter 'from the top down'. We take on so much from our environment, so if adults in a home have high self-esteem, speaking, thinking and behaving in positive, affirming ways, the chances are the children will too.

Sometimes we have to take a step back and actually listen to the way we speak to our children as though we are an objective third party, so we can really understand the messages we regularly give them. For example, you might think nothing of saying 'Don't be so silly,' but if repeated enough, a child will start to believe that they are fundamentally 'silly' or stupid and this will negatively affect their self-esteem. We tend to take our feelings out on those closest to us, but remember that children often don't have the emotional empathy to understand that you are snapping at them because you had a stressful day at work. Both the words and the tone you use will have an impact and should be kept positive wherever possible.

Remember to praise your child, not only for a job well done, but also for the effort they have put in, whilst always remaining truthful. For example, if your child doesn't make the school football team, avoid saying 'Well next time you will have to work harder and you might make it,' but instead say 'Well, you didn't make the team this time but I am really proud of all the effort you have put in.' This way, your child will not only learn how to deal with failure gracefully, but also receive the message that they do not always have to be the best at everything they do.

Remember to reward for effort and completion, rather than outcome. It's important to remember that sometimes a child's skill level just isn't there, but with high self-esteem comes an acceptance of what we are good at, what we are not so good at and what makes us unique.

Don't try to make your child into something they are not. All children have their own strengths and weaknesses. A lot of children feel that they have to live up to their parents' expectations of them, rather than developing the skills that they are naturally good at and enjoy. This is particularly true of teenagers – this is the time when young people need to start forming their own goals and ambitions and should not be striving for the ones that you set for them. Parents sometimes (either consciously or unconsciously) compete using their children's grades and achievements. Children are usually aware of this and receive the message that they must keep up with their peers. Part of having high self-esteem is realising that it is okay to be different and that is something that will come first and foremost from you.

Having realistic standards is a way to maintain high levels of self-esteem. As a parent, you need to be astute to your child's irrational beliefs about themselves, whether these beliefs are about perfection, attractiveness, ability or anything else. It's important to help them to set more accurate standards and be more realistic in evaluating themselves, so they have an accurate concept of themselves and others. For example, a child who does very well in school, but struggles with maths, might say 'I can't do maths, I'm a rubbish student.' Not only is this an inaccurate generalisation, it can become ingrained as a belief that sets children up for future failure. If you hear your child say something like this, try responding with 'You are a great student and do really well in school. Maths is just a subject that you might need to spend a bit more time on.'

Obviously, when a child is very young they are likely to spend more time with you, but as they grow into teenagers it is important for their development that they explore relationships with friends. This helps to develop a sense of independence and identity and also work out their own personal values and beliefs. Communication plays a huge part in building and keeping a strong relationship during this period.

It's important to stay connected and up to date with what your children are doing and who they're doing it with, but *try to do this from a distance, so they do not feel coddled or smothered. The analogy that is often used is of a 'general on the hill' during battle. Imagine your child is on a battlefield – if you go down into the field and fight alongside them you have no clear idea of what they are facing, because you are experiencing challenges contemporaneously with them. If, however, you take a step back into the position of overseeing but not interfering, not only do you have a clear view but, with any luck, your little soldier will come to you for advice if and when they need it.*

The teenage years are when many young people begin to transfer their emotional dependency outside their family, through close friendships and romantic relationships, and sometimes there are disastrous and painful results. They often give up a great deal of themselves in pursuit of the closeness they are craving, only to crash against the hard reality that other teenagers haven't developed the mental facilities to offer them the support they need. Whilst you may feel that you are not at the top of your son or daughter's list of priorities, please remember to regularly reinforce the idea that they can come to you with any discussion, at any time, keeping the lines of communication open even as they stretch their wings outside of the family unit.

Remember also that 'quality time' is more than simply being in the same place at the same time. Often, families can occupy the same physical space without really connecting at all. Engaging with your child means really listening and reacting to whatever it is they have to say and even a little of this goes a very long way in reminding them that they are valued.

It can be difficult after a long day, or when you are feeling stressed, tired or in desperate need of your own quiet time, but taking the time to ask your child what they have been doing and allowing them to talk freely will do wonders for their self-esteem. When they tell you something, show them how interesting they are and ask them to tell you more. Make sure that it is clear that whatever interests them interests you, even if you find it boring or completely incomprehensible. When they speak to you, stop what you are doing, look them in the eye and don't interrupt. This shows you are listening. You might also wish to make a conscious effort to turn off your mobile phone and other outside distractions.

When your child is talking to you, avoid angry or impatient body language such as rolling your eyes or sighing, even if you find what they are saying exasperating, as this will cause them to clam up. Appreciate that your teenager might not have the same views as you, particularly on things like politics, but that sarcasm, confrontation and criticism might just further entrench these views, as it will cause them to be defensive.

However your child tells you they are feeling, accept this at face value. If, for example, they say they are feeling sad, don't try and persuade them that they are not, or force them to cheer up. It's important to recognise and experience negative feelings so we can fully let them go.

If you want to confront an issue with your child, it's better to explain how you are feeling than to point out the flaws in their behaviour. For example, rather than saying 'You never tell me where you are going,' thus pointing the finger at them you could try saying 'I really worry about you when I don't know where you are.' By taking back some of the responsibility, you will encourage your child to open up to you.

There are a couple of prime opportunities to approach any

kind of conversation with a teenager. There are family meal times, although these can feel like more of a formal setting if your child is not used to them. If you are being used as a taxi service, ferrying your child to and from events, you might find this is a good opportunity for a chat. As you are both facing forward, this takes some of the pressure out of the conversation and your child also knows that they are in the car for a finite amount of time so they won't glaze over, anticipating that the conversation will last forever. Another good time is when a teenager returns from a night out. They will be elated from the fun they have been having and much more open to talking, particularly if you have chips in the oven!

Depending on the character of your child, they might really appreciate you taking them for a coffee, or shopping, or to see a film. Some teenagers find the idea of an outing with their parents really embarrassing, whereas others will relish the one-on-one time spent in an activity which is especially for them.

If you suspect there is something wrong with your child or you think they are being bullied, rather than say to them 'Are you being bullied?', try approaching the subject gently, saying that they don't seem to be themselves lately, you are worried about them and asking them if there is anything you can help them with.

Create a safe, loving environment at home. This does not mean unconditionally accepting any behaviour. Boundaries must be set and what is and is not acceptable clearly stated. However much they might protest otherwise, all children like a few rules – they make them feel safe and secure. It's also important, however, to make it clear to your child that it's okay if they make mistakes.

SLEEP

There is a close relationship between sleep and mental health. Many people who experience mental health issues also experience disturbed sleep patterns or insomnia. Over a long period of time, disturbed sleep can actually lead to a mental health problem or make an existing mental health issue worse.

'I suffered with insomnia during my anxiety phase and it made things worse. Your brain is cloudy and foggy and it doesn't allow you to think rationally about anything.'
Tea, 34

Lack of sleep can lead to:
> *Struggling to deal with everyday life*
> *Reduced ability to deal with difficult situations*
> *Lowered self-esteem through inability to cope*
> *Feelings of loneliness*
> *Inability to carry out usual social activities through fatigue*
> *Social isolation*
> *Depression/anxiety*
> *Low mood*
> *Lowered energy levels*

Lack of sleep can also be a symptom of many common mental illnesses, particularly depression, so the situation can become 'chicken and egg'.

Most importantly, being tired can affect your ability to rationalise anxieties and banish irrational thoughts. This can feed into negative thinking patterns which are often associated with poor mental health.

Sleep is not just time out from our busy routine, we all need sleep to help both our minds and bodies recover from the stresses of everyday life. Sleep is a healing process. I'm a great believer that people who are battling negative thoughts or mental health issues can help to recharge their mind by having a small nap during the day. This helps to clear the mind (although the issue shouldn't be forced, as insomnia can be a touchy subject for those experiencing it).

'I find it is particularly hard to maintain a positive outlook when I haven't slept well. I get angry or offended easily and my enthusiasm to participate in things I usually enjoy, like exercise, is dampened.' *Jess, 31*

Getting a good night's sleep is crucial and there are things we can do to help us along to achieving this. Getting into a routine of going to sleep and waking up at the same time is ideal, although not realistic for everyone. A pre-bed routine, which might include having a bath, or reading for half an hour, therefore getting the mind into a relaxed state, will help you drift off better.

For teenagers, a big part of the reason they might be experiencing disturbed sleep is use of technology in the bedroom. Going to bed and then spending time on social media stimulates the brain, making them more likely to wake up in the night (and probably check their accounts again). iPads, smart phones and even television are not recommended for the bedroom.

Make sure bedrooms are as dark and quiet as possible and that the temperature is comfortably cool (but not cold).

Some people find it helpful to imagine a snow plough in their minds' eye, which sweeps aside those niggling anxieties and thoughts which are keeping them awake. This is a very basic form of meditation, which is another way to ensure the brain is in a relaxed state.

Alcohol and caffeine can also disturb sleep, as does eating rich food late at night.

CONCLUSION

Whilst all of this sounds very idealistic, I completely appreciate you and your family are not going to be able to live like the Waltons 100 per cent of the time. The above guidelines are simply to be kept in mind. The way we phrase things and the times we chose to tackle various situations are key in determining how successful the outcome of our conversations. If you can introduce a just few good habits into your family routine, time permitting, it can have a dramatic impact on how your children feel about themselves. In turn, this can improve your own self-esteem as a parent, which will filter down to your children as discussed at the beginning of the chapter and what you are left with is a positive circle of behaviour.

Natasha

CREATING A HIGH SELF-ESTEEM ENVIRONMENT AT SCHOOL

There is, in my experience, something peculiar to the British condition that makes it difficult for us to 'do' feelings. We've made some progress in this area (if only in a sort-of 'I'm singing this for my dead budgie', boxed-up, synthetic, Leona-Lewis-track-in-the-background, X Factor sort of way) but we still seemingly find it impossible to form simple sentences like '*I'm struggling with this.*'

This is hardly surprising, when I think about all the times I have been genuinely distressed about something important and been told by the World to shut up because my feelings are ugly, or embarrassing or inappropriate. For someone with an overdeveloped sense of fairness like, for example, me and **every** teenager who has ever walked this planet, being told your feelings aren't worthy or important makes you feel like you've just been physically crushed. You can't even breathe properly, you're so brimming with indignation at the injustice of it all.

Over time, emotions that aren't expressed fester and become toxic. And here's the thing most people don't know – emotions are impossible to squash. Every time someone has said to you '*Try and put it out of your mind,*' they were asking you to do the impossible. Unacknowledged, feelings will still find a way to seep out, but will no longer be an understandable response to the immediate situation at hand. Anger becomes bitterness. Sadness becomes depression. Jealousy becomes resentment.

Like most things in life that suck, swallowing one's feelings and slapping on a happy, or at least neutral, face is a habit most people have become accustomed to unconsciously. It probably happens during all those times when we're toddlers with no sense of social decorum, raging, tantrumming or weeping in public places, being told by our parents to 'SSSSSHHHH' because we're getting on everyone's nerves. By the time they get to about nine or ten years old, most children will cover their faces with their hands or avert their heads when they cry, because they have learned that raw emotion is something to be ashamed of.

Now, I'm not for one second suggesting that the world would

be a better place if we all went around wailing in each other's faces with wild abandon every time someone forgot to add an extra shot into our skinny lattes. That's no way to get stuff done. Equally, however, we have to see the inherent lunacy in consistently telling a young person that they mustn't express how they feel because it isn't appropriate, then one day demanding that they find the emotional vocabulary to tell us **exactly** how they feel because they've started cutting themselves.

Good communication does not, contrary to popular belief, involve sitting down and earnestly gazing into each other's eyes whilst endlessly raking up fleeting but significant moments from our formative childhood years in the style of the cast of *Dawson's Creek*. It can actually be achieved by something as simple as asking someone how their day was, or what they think about that, or what they meant when they said that. And it's something that, crucially, has to be nurtured consistently.

You can instantly tell when you walk into an environment where people's feelings and opinions are valued – be it a home, a school or a work place. They're usually the places where everyone's smiling and getting on with what they're supposed to be doing in a productive manner.

I see it all the time in schools. My heart always sinks when, before I'm due to address an assembly, a form tutor or Head of Year gets up to do a little speech about how my audience *must be on their best behaviour* because they are *representing the school*. This will usually be followed by some fist-munchingly patronising phrase like '*Now I know you* ***can*** *behave because I have seen you do it before,*' as though otherwise their default mode would be to start flinging themselves on top of one another, biting each other's ears off and howling like beasts. I'm then faced with the task of spending the first ten minutes of the session persuading the year group that it's okay to express an authentic emotion in response to the lesson.

For the record, neither I nor any of my team have ever taken 'good' or 'bad' behaviour of individual students as an indicator of the quality of a school. There will inevitably be some teenagers with a longer attention span than others, there's always the 'class clown' and the cool kid who is desperate to convey how utterly unbothered they are by the subject matter at hand. It has been this way since teenagers were invented, circa thirteen years and nine months after Adam and Eve had their first shag. It's our job to engage these students in a way that's meaningful to them.

A school's character **can** be defined, however, by the attitude of the staff towards the students and this is something I'm always careful to take note of. In fact, I am giving serious consideration to compiling my own 'Schools Guide' as an alternative to those huge tomes you can buy that say things like *'This school has a swimming pool and 60 per cent of its pupils get an A at GCSE.'* I think it's far more important to know *'This school has the sort of environment that will encourage your children to be confident enough to expose their bodies and actually use the sodding swimming pool and staff who will nurture your child's unique skills and potential, even if they're never going to get an A at GCSE.'*

It really is fascinating, the discrepancy between how a school is generally viewed within a community or a league table and what you witness within its walls. I should say at this juncture that the vast majority of the schools I've been into, by virtue of the fact that they're the sorts of places that would have someone like me come in to speak to the students, are fantastic. There have, however, been a few notable exceptions.

Every year, for some unfathomable reason, I'm invited to a school in Hertfordshire that is the most oppressively awful educational institution you could ever think of. The lack of aspiration and inspiration is actually palpable in the air within its walls. It's all gloomy and grey and crusty and everyone looks as though they're contemplating suicide. I always like to ask the cabbie who takes me from the station to the school what the school is like (cabbies usually being able to provide a view which is sometimes terrifyingly or otherwise refreshingly devoid of any regard for political correctness). According to local cabbies, this school is in a 'good area', the children there come from middle class families, making it *by no means the worst school in the county*'. Which just goes to prove that the automatic link we tend to make between academic excellence and affluence might not be as strong as we think.

I could not understand why the school insisted on re-issuing their invitation to me each year because as far as I could see I was having no impact on the pupils whatsoever. Every time, they entered the room as though they have had the life sucked out of them, then proceed to sit, zombie-like, while their Year Head lectured them on the importance of *being quiet*. I've never been able to raise a laugh, a gasp, a '*No way!*' – none of the usual range of emotions I get when presenting my talk – from these particular young people. They would just sit and stare at me with wide, sad eyes, like the puppies you see in adverts for the RSPCA.

One year I happened to turn up with more than half an hour to spare before my lesson was due to begin. Usually when this happens, a smiley Head of PSHE will come and say hello, ask me how my journey was and offer me a cup of tea, as dictated by the Big Rulebook of British Good Manners. In this instance, an incredibly surly Head of Year came storming into reception, looked at me as though I was the last person on Earth she wanted to see at that moment, sighed, said *'You're early'* in an accusatory manner before declaring *'You'd better come and sit in the staffroom. We're having lunch.'*

Being granted access to the staffroom suddenly brought this school and all its difficulties into the realms of a non-enigma. I sat, completely ignored, in the corner as I listened to teachers bemoan the *'little shits'* they taught and what they perceived to be the prison-like environs in which they worked. One cannot perform one's best academically if one strongly suspects that the person educating one wishes one would *'just fuck off and die.'* FACT.

I know being a teacher is incredibly hard. Sometimes, when I get home after having had to repeat the same lesson, with the same amount of energy and enthusiasm to different audiences eight times in a row, I marvel at the way teachers do that job every day **and** find the requisite energy to plan lessons and mark coursework. I can imagine it is intense and draining and thankless (because everyone wrongly believes you to be jammy bastards that clock off at 3pm on the dot and have six weeks unencumbered holiday every summer). But if you don't at the very least like young people, teaching is probably not for you. As far as I can see, teaching is a profession which regularly involves being so knackered you can hardly see but is ultimately rendered worth it by the notion that you have imparted wisdom in some form to a person who needs it. They should put that at the top of the description of teacher training courses.

I can honestly say that, in the event that I am lucky enough to be blessed with my own little Devons, I would rather give up my job and home school them than send them to that school in Hertfordshire. Which would prove rather disastrous for them if they showed any sort of inclination towards maths or geography, both of which I can conclusively say I'm terrible at. I'm therefore pleased that this particular school is not indicative of 'the norm', in my experience.

Conversely, one of the best schools I've ever been to is in Croydon, South London. It's one of the few schools where I consented to work with year 7s prior to us developing a lesson specifically for younger pupils, when the content of our lessons was universally fairly grown-up. Even the eleven year olds there are spectacularly well-rounded, empathetic, switched-on human beings whose level of maturity, let's face it, far exceeds my own. The pupils there have so much passion for life and for just knowing new things and being able to have an opinion on them that, when I remember them, they seemed to be sparkling with the force of it.

I walked across the school grounds with one of the teachers between lessons on a Monday morning and noticed how many pupils actually stopped to engage **her** in conversation. *'How was your weekend, Miss?'* some of them asked and one even said *'You know that thing we were doing on Friday, Miss? Well I was thinking...'* which is the best thing a student can **ever** say to their teacher. If you've inspired your students to apply what they have learned in your classroom to the outside world then you officially rock as an educator. I wanted to give the teacher a cuddle but I thought she might find it strange.

When we reached the Head Teacher's office I made a point

of telling her how impressed I was by the relationship between staff and pupils there, which seemed both natural and respectful. Then I sort of lost my shit a little bit and forgot to display the appropriate amount of decorum for the environs of a Head Teacher's office because I was too excited to be there and see education working in such a harmonious and effective way.

'*HOW? How are you doing this!? How do you get your pupils to be so amazing without even trying?*' I demanded (arms flailing about wildly as they tend to do when I'm feeling particularly impassioned).

'*Well, it's quite simple really,*' the Head replied with a wry smile. '*We like them.*'

CHAPTER 7

BULLYING

Natasha

Next door to my former all-girl secondary school on the Essex border there is a Victorian style house with bay windows. I'm fairly certain it's been bought by someone now, but back in the day seniors were allowed to use it at break and lunch times as a gigantic, two-tiered common room. Which was, obviously, awesome.

As was always going to happen, rooms were immediately allocated according to our inter-school social hierarchy. The two largest rooms on the ground floor were 'bagsied' by the cool-but-scary mob and their still-cool-but-not-quite-so-scary sub-group. Upstairs, there were the boffins in one room and then the 'quite-boffy-but-also-prone-to-daft-Monty-Python-style-humour-and-regular-hysterical-giggles' girls (of which I was a fully paid-up member). Goths and musos tended to hang out in the kitchen because there was a stereo in there. And there was a special corner where sexually active sixth formers went to do heavy petting.

The cool-but-scary group consisted of about twelve girls, all of whom had boyfriends with cars, were really good at sport despite the fact they smoked and used to punch people in the arm a lot for no apparent reason. They used to leave the door of their room open and shout scathing comments at whoever happened to walk past. Since you had to walk past their room to enter and exit the house, their comments were directed at pretty much everyone.

I remember when my boobs materialised out of nowhere aged sixteen (seriously, I woke up one morning and had gigantic boobs) they'd shout '*It's rude to point!*', in acknowledgement of the fact that I hadn't yet found a bra that would disguise my nipples. They'd also regularly ask me if I was pregnant before collapsing with laughter (because my tummy stuck out. You see? HILARIOUS). Once, they seized upon the idea that my friend and I were lesbians and for about a month insisted on doing that finger-vagina-tongue gesture at us. They'd also do things like leave money on the pavement outside and then shout '*SKANK!*' out of the window if anyone tried to pick it up.

Now, it seemed quite obvious to me even at the time that these girls were, for want of a better phrase, Artless Dicks. I can't say anything they said or did ever unduly bothered me. Sometimes, I even thought it was quite funny (if only in a sort of 'Artless Dick' type way).

Recently, I bumped into another member of the 'Boff-Monty-Python Crew' and she said '*Oh God, remember how that lot downstairs used to bully us **horrifically**?*' She then told me that quite often she used to walk right past our room upstairs, lock herself in the broom cupboard and cry for ten minutes before coming in.

It was then that it dawned on me – the severity of bullying is impossible to categorise from the outside. I would not automatically describe those girls as 'bullies' but clearly, in the eyes of my friend, they were.

What does strike me is this – something about the way my friend perceived herself made her more sensitive and susceptible to outside influence. We are back to self-esteem again. I loved school and was popular (although mostly with teachers, but that was fine because they knew interesting stuff and had the key to the cupboard where the KitKats were kept). When I was at school I was in my element. My self-esteem was sky high. Comments designed to be hurtful that were made within its walls would bounce off me, largely unacknowledged. If I had been more vulnerable, these actions might have had a lasting impact.

This is not to be misconstrued as 'victim blaming'. I believe we should always work on the basis that some people are more vulnerable than others and try to be as kind as we can. It's merely an illustration of the vital nature of high self-esteem in diminishing the impact of bullying.

INTERVIEW WITH RACHEL BEDDOE, AUTHOR OF *SURVIVING GIRLHOOD* AND TEAM MEMBER AT CARDIFF AGAINST BULLYING

I met Rachel at a conference for teaching professionals in Cardiff and immediately identified her as someone who has the same ethos when it comes to young people and education. '*Don't talk down to them*' is more often than not Rachel's mantra and for this reason she has been hugely successful delivering PSHE lessons in her native Wales.

Rachel has studied bullying and its effect on teenagers extensively and is always writing and saying extremely wise things on the subject, some of which are below:

Q: What actually defines bullying?
You have to look at whatever is going on from two different perspectives – that of the perpetrator and that of the target. What was the intention behind the action and what was the target's perception of that intention? If the perpetrator didn't intend to cause harm then you have to consider what is going on in the target's life that made them feel bullied in that situation.

Q: What are the signs parents should look for that might indicate their child is being bullied?
Any kind of change in behaviour, in particular if they become either unusually withdrawn or aggressive.

Other indicators would be if they are not sleeping well, if they avoid certain places or regularly claim to have unexplained illnesses in order to avoid going to school. Truancy and bullying often go hand in hand. Then of course there are unexplained marks on the body which can indicate that they are being physically abused.

Often, when a young person is being bullied they will try to ask you about it by telling third person stories. They might say for example 'My friend is going through this, what do you think they should do?'

Q: Online bullying is now a huge issue amongst children and young people. Are there any specific signs which might point to this?

In addition to all of the above, look out for their use of technology. Bizarrely, a young person's use of social media etc. will usually increase if they are being bullied. If they are always looking at their phone or using it late at night this might point to them being targeted by online bullies.

Q: What about if your child is the one perpetrating the bullying? How would parents know and what should they do?

Be aware of the way your child talks about people, noting whether it is negative or positive. If their tone is very aggressive, they might be bullying. You might also receive complaints from other people, for example teachers or the parents of the child who is being bullied.

If you suspect your child is bullying others, it's important to keep calm when you talk to them about it. Reassure them that it's not them, but their behaviour which is the problem and needs to change and that you still love them. You are there specifically to address the behaviour. Any confrontation or shouting is likely to make them clam up or become defensive.

Q: What steps can we take to protect those who are being bullied?

Again, it is important that you don't get emotional and remain calm. Listen – let them tell you their story without interrupting.

Encourage them to come up with their own solution by asking them what they would like to see happen. You can make suggestions at this point but don't overtly tell them what to do.

Parents shouldn't inform the school unless they have the consent of the child to do so. You should try and encourage them to give this consent and make sure they know how important it is that the school is aware of what is going on.

Q: A recent survey revealed that one third of people believe that bullying is 'character building' and therefore not too much of a problem. What would you say to those people?

Bullying is without question a form of abuse and it can go on to affect you into your adulthood. We can see the effects of bullying behaviour that took place in formative years in adults both at work and in their social and romantic lives. Targets will always see themselves as victims. They are likely to become very defensive, or withdrawn or depressed. The same survey showed that half of all people bullied at school go on to develop clinical depression.

As for those who bully – unless their behaviour is challenged right away they will still think it is okay to treat people like this as they make their way into adulthood.

Bullying isn't a rite of passage and every effort should be made to stop it as soon as it is detected.

Q: Anything else you'd like to add?

Parents and teachers should know that bullying should never be brushed to one side. It's really important to get to the bottom of what the root causes are and to address those root causes. The behaviour will stop once those root causes are sorted out.

Some examples of root causes are bereavement, family issues, lack of resilience, jealousy and lack of confidence. No one bullies because they have high self-esteem so it is important that both the bully and the person being bullied get the help they need.

CHAPTER 8

SEXUALITY AND SELF-ESTEEM

Natasha

When people reminisce about their teenage years, they'll usually begin by telling you about their first crush, a fledgling romance that happened during that time, or how little attention they got from the objects of their desires. Our sexual awakening, happening as it does concurrent with a period when we are working out who we are in every other aspect of our lives, is an important component in our self-esteem.

Dr David Bainbridge, who is a lecturer in Reproductive Biology at Cambridge University (and a Very Clever Man) has this to say on the topic:

Whether we like it or not in our modern, politically correct world, the drive to want other people and to be wanted by other people is at the centre of who we are. Coupling is such a strong urge that it remains strong in homosexual people, and even heterosexual people who do not want children. Although we may not like the idea, developing a sense of sexuality is a key part of children's growth and self-belief.

Having our sexuality validated by the world confirms to us that we are acceptable. Similarly, being made to feel ashamed of our sexual desires can go on to impact our personal development.

This clearly goes beyond the traditional remit of Sex Ed. This is not about young people having the sort of relationship with their elders whereby they feel confident to ask whether it's normal for sex to last forty-eight seconds and what to do if the condom splits. This is more about who they are when they're shagging (or thinking about it) and recognising that, whoever that person might be, they are a reflection of who they are the rest of time (or who they wish they were). If we're going to talk about self-esteem, we almost certainly have to acknowledge the importance of sex.

This is problematic for family and teachers, for a couple of reasons. First of all, any young person will have a bit of an 'ick TMI!' ('Too Much Information') default response if their relations or teachers give them even the merest inkling of a hint that they might have entertained the notion of getting jiggy. Similarly, parents and teachers don't want to look at their adorable young charges in their little school uniforms and contemplate the fact that they might be having sexual thoughts of their own (because that is also a bit ick). Yet we clearly cannot leave young people to discuss such matters within their own peer groups because:

a. Anyone whose tastes fall outside the norm is going to get the piss ripped out of them and that might lead of them feeling ashamed of their sexual desires, and therefore themselves, for years to come.

b. Today's teenagers' expectations of what constitutes 'normal' sexual desire is almost entirely defined by online pornography.

c. Have you ever heard teenagers discussing sex? It's terrifying how much misinformation they manage to glean. I heard them talking about ear sex once. **Ear sex.** Is that even a thing?

So what can we do? The first thing we can do is impress upon young people the fact that almost all representations of sex, whether fed to us by Hollywood or from books (I'm looking at you, *Twilight*) bear no resemblance to the actual act and represent only a tiny spectrum of human desire. Even internet porn, which theoretically covers a huge range of sexual tastes, doesn't generally encompass emotion or set the act within the context of a caring relationship. So nothing they see or read is going to prepare them, realistically. In doing so we give responsibility for their sexual journey back to the young person. We tell them that they do not have to be pale imitations of what they see on page or screen.

The second thing we can do is make young people feel entitled enough to say no to the sexual acts they are not comfortable with and to explore the possibility of things they might want to try. Fortunately, this does not involve directly addressing the specifics of their sexual preferences (phew!). By raising self-esteem generally and reassuring young people that their feelings and wishes are valued, we encourage safe and healthy sexual practice by proxy.

If, however, your child, student or family member does want to unburden themselves and speak to you about their sexual tastes, it's important to respond in the correct way. This is something I learned unwittingly by doing it completely wrong.

About two years ago, a friend told me he enjoyed wearing women's clothes, mostly during sex, but sometimes in other situations, too. I responded in what I thought was the right way, by telling him how I felt: which was nothing whatsoever. It didn't affect the way I perceived him as a friend and as a liberal person I don't consider it any of my business what goes on between two consenting adults. So I just said something along the lines of 'Okay. Whatever.' A year later, I had the revelation that I could have handled it better, thanks to a discussion with a Sex Coach called Faerie...

My editor at Cosmo asked me if I wanted to go to a 'Sex Workshop' and write about my experience for the readers. (To which my response was 'Of course I bloody do!') In my mind, I expected to enter some sort of bright pink neon, vagina-crossed-with-nightclub type space and have to demonstrate my hand-job technique on a dildo to a room full of strangers. Whilst not exactly my idea of a good Friday night, I do love it when I'm given the opportunity to do something completely outrageous and comfort-zone shattering vicariously, in the name of journalism.

So imagine my surprise when I found myself in a cosy North London flat with Faerie and a lady who looked a bit like Trudy Styler, sitting on floor cushions with about twelve other (fantastically lovely) people discussing the implications of sexual desire, whilst eating flapjacks. That was genuinely my idea of a good Friday night. Except it was a Tuesday.

As a heterosexual woman whose tastes meander only into the most socially acceptable forms of kinky, I'd never given much thought to what it might be like to have to explore the meanings behind your sexual preferences and then attempt to have them recognised and accepted by the world. Everyone accepts my sexual preferences (with the possible exception of people who don't believe in sex before marriage).

Of course I'd considered what it must be like to grow up as a gay or bisexual person and how isolating an experience that might be, when we tend to make the assumption that everyone is heterosexual until otherwise stated. But I'd never considered all the many, many other ways there are to have a sexual identity and the impact that might have on self-esteem.

Faerie told us about how an insistent curiosity about BDSM (bondage, domination, sadism & masochism) when he was a straight-laced, married 'corporate bod' called Justin, led him to completely change a life he felt stifled by. He left his job and his marriage, explored his sexual horizons by travelling the world and has now found happiness in his new identity, lifestyle and profession. For Faerie, his sexuality was the key to unlocking who he really was.

As Faerie told his story, I realised what I should have said to my friend. I should have said '*I think it's brilliant that you enjoy doing that.*' I should have made it clearer that I wasn't merely indifferent or even casually accepting of his sexuality, but that I actively embraced it. When he told me about his preferences, he was actually asking me to recognise a significant part of who he, my friend, truly is.

That's why 'coming out' to family is so significant, not only because of the relationships we might have in the future (and therefore who might go on to become part of our family) but because we as humans have a visceral need to know that the people we love love us back unconditionally.

I have kept in touch with Faerie (for no other reason than I think he is cool) and asked him what he perceived to be the relationship between sexuality and self-esteem. He said:

> As we start to explore our unique and precious sexuality, we begin meeting all the things that are inside us: our desires, our fantasies, our passions and our longings. Whether our tastes are more mainstream or further out, there is a direct link between how much we embrace our sexuality and how we feel about ourselves. Without a healthy acceptance of our sexuality it's very hard for us to move into positive self-regard and high self-esteem.

I have always felt it would be irresponsible of me to try and shoe-horn something as complex and multi-faceted as sexuality into my lesson on body image and self-esteem. It is only one hour, after all. However, it is often apparent from the questions I am asked afterwards that the students have made their own connection between the class content and their sexual identity.

On a couple of occasions, I have met teenagers who feel as though they have been born into the wrong gender. This is probably the most extreme example of a case where drastically modifying the body would be a pursuit in 'being yourself'. That's why it's really important not to condemn things like plastic surgery – because for every thousand women who think they need to get a boob job to make themselves more acceptable to the patriarchy there is a person bravely defying social conditioning by reconstructing their bodies to more accurately reflect their identity. I'll go on to talk more about focusing on motivation rather than action in the body image chapter, next.

I have noticed that generally (although not always) gay female students seem to be less affected by media-imposed beauty paradigms (although are often far more angry about them) and gay men are more concerned with conforming to conventional notions of attractiveness (although heterosexual men are fast catching them up in this regard).

Fellow journalist, purveyor of sweary opinions and good friend of mine Jake Basford writes for a number of LGBT (Lesbian Gay Bisexual and Transgender) publications and is gay himself. I asked him why he thought gay men might be more concerned with personal aesthetics. He said:

It's essentially peer pressure. When you talk to gay men on their own, quite often they secretly really hate this idea that we're all supposed to be buff and hairless and groomed to perfection all the time. But in groups, we'll compete about who's going to the gym. Well. I mean, I don't. I tell them all to shut the fuck up and go to the bar for another vodka, but other gay men do.

Jake also has a really interesting theory when it comes to the link between homosexuality and self-esteem:

> *As soon as you come out you are lumped into several boxes, because that is the way the LGBT community works – you are judged on age, race, sexual orientation (ironically), weight, hairiness, sexual habits, sero-status, music taste, and lot's more besides right down to whether you prefer to go to a pub or a wine bar. For a group of the population that hates being judged, we love imposing that regime internally, and what this means in terms of body image, therefore, is that you have wave upon wave of hypocritical attitudes and ridiculously high expectations when it comes to our bodies.*

I wonder whether perhaps, having inevitably felt isolated for so long growing up outside the accepted social 'identity' is what compels the LGBT community to then want to categorise each other so stringently? Perhaps there is a comfort in knowing with which LGBT faction you belong, having felt that you do not 'belong' during your formative years.

Indeed, the recurring theme which runs through all the research I've conducted into sexuality is the incessant need we have as humans to label. It's built into us that we must 'have the measure' of each other so we can know where we sit in the pecking order of any social or professional situation. It's a caveman-esque instinct and, much like the desire to wear animal fur and club each other over the noggins, it is an instinct that must be fought.

When it comes to sexuality, labelling young people stifles

them. It creates the expectation that we will fit into neat little boxes, when in fact sexuality is something very unique, diverse and as Faerie says, precious.

I have lost count of the number of times I have read on the problem pages in magazines for teenage girls '*I'm having sexual feelings for my female best mate, does that mean I'm gay?*' It always strikes me that the writer is less concerned with the feelings they are experiencing and more worried about the implication for how they should label themselves. We need to reassure young people that everyone, and we mean **everyone**, thinks about sex with people of the same gender at some point in their lives. It may eventually transpire that they are gay or bisexual, or it might not. Either way that's okay, but for the time being they are perfectly entitled just to take some time working things out. After all, our sexuality constantly evolves throughout our lives, we can't be expected to tick a box and stick to it by the age of sixteen.

Giving young people space to explore notions of sexuality and gender is essential. It's important that we make it clear that there is more than one way to have an intimate relationship. The expectation, not only of heterosexuality, but that they will automatically get married and reproduce, weighs heavily on lots of young people. Subconsciously, we reinforce those expectations all the time using language. We should think carefully before we make statements which assume everyone is the same.

Recently, I saw in a staffroom literature from Stonewall, a campaign group which promotes equality for lesbians, gay men and bisexuals. There was a leaflet for each school subject (e.g. Maths, Science, English, History) with suggestions on how

125

teachers can casually incorporate the notion of homosexuality and bisexuality within the context of that lesson.

This strikes me as a really very sensible way to approach sexuality within education. Quite often, a student who has been identified as having an eating disorder will ask to be excused from my body image class. This might seem strange, since the subject matter is so obviously relevant to them, but it's born out of the potential crashing humiliation of a one hundred and fifty-strong year group all being aware that they have been called together to address something going on in the life of one of them. They are terrified of the scrutiny that would bring. (Usually in these cases I'll have a chat with the student beforehand and reassure them that it's a universally relevant lesson for anyone who has a body and that I won't single them out or force them to participate).

Similarly, having one giant assembly on sexuality might make LGBT students feel singled out and therefore have the opposite effect to the one intended. Although I do agree it's very important to have PSHE lessons on topics such as homophobic bullying, I also think the reality that there have always been and continue to be LGBT people can be gently and regularly reinforced in other lessons, to make it less of a big deal (and probably, as a result, also reduce homophobic bullying).

In essence, the aim is to drive home the notion that we are individuals and young people can tailor their sexual needs to what feels right for them, rather than having them dictated by society's linear parameters. Or, as Jake puts it:

Having been through the coming out and growing up gay thing, the only recommendation to give is to listen to Shirley Bassey: 'Life is a sham 'til you can shout out I am what I am.'

CHAPTER 9

BODY IMAGE

Natasha

There are two misapprehensions I have constantly struggled with during my time as a body image campaigner. The first is that body image isn't really significant in comparison to other 'important' things and therefore issues arising out it only befall the vacuous and vain. The second is that body image is only relevant to women and girls.

I shall dispel these myths now:

BODY IMAGE AS A 'FLUFFY' SUBJECT

There are two times of year where my services as a body-image pundit for radio and television are particularly in demand – summer and Christmas. These are, lest we forget, times when people are likely to be away from work. Half the media and most of Parliament have fucked off on their holibobs. Those remaining are left scratching around for something to present to the public as 'news'. So that's when body image has its moment in the headlines, in between pieces about tennis, hayfever and (ironically) endless articles on how to get a 'bikini body' or sidestep inevitable weight gain during the festive season. They're times when current affairs generally becomes lighter in feel, major diplomatic world events notwithstanding.

Despite this context, my Twitter feed is always invaded by at least a dozen blustering protestors per media appearance, who wonder why we are wasting valuable air time discussing something so utterly meaningless when the ozone layer is melting/pandas are becoming extinct/plastic bags are now costing us 5p a pop. There is still a commonly held belief that body image doesn't really matter. Which would be really irritating if I wasn't either too hot to muster the requisite energy to be angry (summer) or already a little bit tipsy having put Baileys on my branflakes that morning (Christmas).

In my opinion, there is no more reliable indicator of what is going on within the confines of a person's mind than how they feel about their body and how inclined they are to look after it. When we are frustrated or dissatisfied, we tend to project those feelings onto the nearest tangible object: our physical selves. Self-harm, eating disorders, exercise addiction, 'comfort' eating, binge drinking – these are all ways in which we punish our bodies for something which, more often than not, has its genesis in the mind. Our bodies are the vessels in which we live our lives. Our relationships with them are therefore paramount in our ability to function effectively.

Body image is not only relevant to those who have a diagnosable body-related issue. Maslow's Hierarchy of Needs is a very useful pyramid, visually depicting the elements human beings need in order to survive and thrive, in order of urgency. Whilst first seen in Maslow's paper '*A Theory of Human Motivation*' in 1943, it is still widely cited as a template for understanding what drives us. Basic considerations like food, shelter and water form the base of the pyramid, followed by safety and a sense of belonging within one's community. The fourth tier of the pyramid is self-esteem. Maslow shows that we need a solid foundation of self-esteem before we're able to turn our attentions to 'self-actualisation', which is the pursuit of talent, creativity and fulfilment (and, I would add, learning). Since body image is both an indicator and a component in self-esteem, it's therefore part of that vital penultimate tier.

Body dissatisfaction has a measureable impact on potential. In 2013, Girlguiding and the Dove Self-Esteem Project conducted a study of young women which revealed that 64 per cent of eleven to sixteen-year-old girls would describe themselves as lacking body confidence. Furthermore, 47 per cent of those surveyed said that the way they felt about their bodies stopped them from partaking in everyday activities undertaken at school, including sports, presenting to the class/drama activities and even raising their hand to ask a question.

The enjoyment of physical activity, ability to present ideas to audiences and most importantly the confidence to question when we do not understand are, any reasonable person would concede, essential life skills. Yet almost half of teenage girls (no equivocal survey has yet been done on teenage boys as far as I'm aware – see below) are missing out on the opportunity to develop those skills because of body related insecurity.

If one doesn't feel able to fully participate in a normal sort of school day, it stands to reason that one will not get the most out of one's education. This has implications for the qualifications one will receive, the decisions one will make about the subjects one will study and ultimately the jobs one will consider oneself capable of.

Yet the ramifications of low-body confidence don't begin and end in school. Endless research has been conducted into the seeming-phenomenon of 'better looking' people attaining higher paid jobs. I would argue that we live in a culture which simply allows conventionally 'good looking' people to feel more comfortable in their own skin, which then gives them the confidence to seek better paid roles. Similarly, it is this same confidence that will cause an employee to be noticed in a working environment and singled out for promotion. It is therefore not how our bodies look, but how proud or ashamed we feel of our physical form which is a component in our success.

Our relationship with our body often informs how entitled we feel – whether that's entitlement to happiness, wealth or even love. We make huge, life-changing decisions based on our perception of how attractive we are and therefore what we 'deserve'.

The link between physical beauty and entitlement is introduced to most of us at an early age. Aside from *Shrek*, I struggle to think of one feature length children's cartoon which does not have a slender, youthful, doe-eyed, Caucasian-ised heroine at its centre and a buff, broad shouldered, square-jawed hero. Plump, less-than-symmetrical characters, or those with disabilities, are relegated to supporting roles. We are given an unequivocal message as children – only the gorgeous are allowed to be the main character in their own lives. This message is constantly reinforced by the society in which we live as we grow older. So it's little surprise that the same Girlguiding/Dove survey found that 87 per cent of teenage girls believe they are judged more on their looks than they are on their ability.

If it was simply a case of dieting and botoxing oneself into an approximation of what society deems beautiful and then getting on with one's life that, whilst deplorable, would at least be a finite, manageable problem. Unfortunately, multi-billion pound fitness, beauty and fashion industries depend upon inventing new body insecurities to occupy our time and worry. They cannot ever allow us to be entirely satisfied with how we look because this diminishes our value as a consumer. Hence beauty paradigms become increasingly extreme throughout history, demanding more and more time, energy and, crucially, cash devoted to attainment and upkeep. I cannot pinpoint exactly when young women began believing that if you do not have a 'thigh gap' this automatically renders you 'fat', or when young men began reinforcing this belief in everyday rhetoric. It's a poignant example of shifting beauty paradigms, however, especially as 'thigh gap surgery' now exists without the plastic surgery industry apparently feeling it necessary to mention that presence or absence of a gap between the thighs is dictated by bone structure and gait, not weight.

A couple of days ago, a friend of mine contacted me for comment on a piece she is writing about earlobe surgery. Yes, you read that correctly. The latest cosmetic surgery trend is for women to have fat injected into their earlobes, because (apparently) as we age our lobes become longer and thinner. That's right, ladies, you can have all the facelifts in Christendom but your ears are going to give your (totally shameful) age away. This is clearly a very urgent problem so thank fuck the medical profession have stepped in to provide a solution (Yes, I'm being sarcastic).

If the very existence of procedures such as toe liposuction (yes, that too is an actual thing) and earlobe surgery doesn't prove that there'll always be a new part of our body we're supposed to apologise for, I don't know what does. The upshot is, unless we develop the ability to question the messages being fired at us constantly by marketing companies, we'll (literally, in some instances) be on that treadmill forever. The pursuit of a beauty ideal whose goal posts will forever be moved takes up a huge amount of what TV presenter and my mate Cherry Healey calls 'Lady Brain Space' (and Man Brain Space too – see below).

So yes, in an ideal world young people should be concerning themselves with more lofty considerations than whether or not they have a six pack, or if there is a gap between their thighs, but unfortunately until we eradicate those concerns there is statistically a lot of untapped potential being wasted.

If body image considerations have the ability to clip the metaphorical wings and narrow the world view of a person, imagine what they are doing to the cumulative potential of the nation. Imagine how many days of work and school are missed, how many promotions not gone for, wages not earned and experiences not had as a direct result of body image worries. Imagine what we might be able to achieve, not just as individuals but as a society, if these body image issues were eradicated.

It's therefore difficult to exaggerate the importance of body image. End of. Never darken my Twitter feed again, ye doubters.

MALE BODY IMAGE

Men have bodies too. They are not heads in jars. Do not be mistaken, teaching body image lessons to young men is a far more arduous and soul-destroying task than it is for their female counterparts. Yet I'm proud to say that we continue to be one of the only UK-based education programmes that offers body image and self-esteem lessons for boys because I believe that, whilst men may be less vocal about their body worries, to some extent they need our help more.

When you try and talk to groups of boys about anything involving emotions or intimacy, they invariably either grunt or laugh. This has been interpreted, certainly in the sphere of body image campaigning, as a lack of interest. In reality, I believe it's because men are so unused to talking about how they feel that they simply don't have the terminology to hand to express it. The grunting or laughing is a reflection of the novelty of the situation. Add to that the constant pressure young men are under to appear 'masculine', they'll often try to demonstrate their lack of interest in the topic, by turning their chairs or heads away from the front of the class or rolling their eyes... But catch them off guard and you will see that you have hit a nerve.

A council once subcontracted to me for a week to deliver body image lessons in their area and asked approximately 650 students to fill in feedback forms so they could assess their effectiveness. The commonest thing written under 'any other comments' by male students was:

'Thank you for asking us what we thought about this.'

Doesn't that make you want to cry? That we're so conditioned by social gender constraints that young men are actually grateful to have the opportunity to give their opinion about something?

Young women, conversely, talk so much about bodies, diets and exercise that they tend to normalise behaviours which are, in reality, completely abnormal. I saw Dr Susie Orbach (author of *Fat is a Feminist Issue*) speak at Parliament, once. (I've never seen such a small person command so much space. She was magnificent. Since then, I've wanted to be her when I grow up). In her speech she spoke about how dieting and exercise practices which would have been classified as serious eating disorders when she first began working as a psychotherapist thirty years ago are now commonly accepted and even advocated. Cutting out entire food groups from the diet, for example, would have once been cause for shock and concern but is now widely practiced and accepted.

The challenge with young women is convincing them that simply because 'everyone' does something does not make it healthy or acceptable. It is also allowing them to see that they are more than the sum of their parts. Their disproportionate compulsion to discuss body image matters means bodies have been taken out of all perspective. With young men, however, there is still a shroud of secrecy which covers anything relating to the body. As a teacher or parent, one faces the opposite challenge of getting them to open up about their feelings and experiences and convincing them that whatever they are going through is normal and nothing to be ashamed of.

That's why, controversially, I always recommend teachers separate boys and girls for body image lessons. (This has the added advantage of meaning the heterosexual students are much less distracted!). Girls do not want to be told what the official definitions of anorexia and bulimia are or be alerted to the fact that airbrushing exists. By the age of twelve most of them are already more than aware of these sorts of things and I have a strict policy against being condescending. Boys, however, invariably still need this basic information, delivered in a way that does not leave them believing these issues only ever affect girls and women. (Of course, there should be an opportunity for them to discuss what they have learned afterwards in tutor groups if they are in a co-educational environment, so they can understand the impact the subject has on their classmates).

Men are about ten years behind women, in terms of their relationships with their bodies. Around one decade ago, it was as though the beauty industry suddenly thought *'Hang on! We're missing out on half our market, here!'* and began very aggressively pursuing men in its marketing. It is no coincidence that during that time diagnosed instances of male eating disorders have risen by a whopping 66 per cent*.

A 2013 survey by Co-Operative Pharmacy revealed that 53 per cent of men aged eighteen to seventy-five would happily describe themselves as 'metrosexual', using products such as moisturiser, fake tan and plucking/tinting their eyebrows. This is, in theory at least, wonderful – I love the idea that men have freedom to experiment with their appearance above and beyond a shower and a shave. Yet I also believe women have a moral obligation to try and protect men from the potentially devastating side-helping of body insecurity which can come from using beauty products and more specifically buying into their advertising methods.

The body image gender playing field is being levelled, but entirely the wrong way. Women should be striving to be as carefree about their 'imperfections' as the majority of men historically have been, not the other way around. It makes me really angry that, as a society, we're just standing by and letting men go through the same vile, self-destructive, anguish-inducing beauty journey women have without (apparently) feeling any need to intervene.

Caryn Franklin, co-founder of the brilliant 'All Walks Beyond the Catwalk' campaign once said, when asked about the gender discrepancy in body image:

'We're all at battle, but women are on the front line.'

I'd put it a different way – women and girls need damage control, but with men and boys there is the potential to do pre-emptive damage limitation, if only we can get our approach right.

If I had to recommend one thing we can do as a society to protect young men, I'd put a strict age limit on when you are able to join a gym, barring exceptional medical circumstances. I would probably recommend eighteen as an appropriate age to start working out in a gym, although I could probably be talked down to sixteen. It is now not at all unusual for me to hear classes of Year 9 boys (thirteen and fourteen years of age) discussing their gym habits. There is absolutely no reason why young men of this age should not be able to engage in physical activity outside a gym environment. I realise of course that Physical Education in state schools has been severely restricted over the past few years, as has funding for sports centres, and that is absolutely not ideal. But everyone can still put on a pair of trainers and go running or play some football in the park. Unless a doctor recommends it, there's no reasonable 'health' argument for gym membership at such an early age.

This is not a tirade against gyms and should not be read as such. In fact, I am a member of one myself and really enjoying working out there. (Well. 'Enjoy' is probably pushing it. I like the endorphins afterwards.) But I'm also aware of the extent to which I am bombarded with attempts to sell me things, as soon as I walk in the front door. Protein shakes, snack bars, additional classes and exercise equipment are advertised via posters and that's before we get into what might be recommended by your fellow gym-goers and personal trainers. As an adult, I trust myself to devise an exercise regime on my own terms, taking the advice that I need and dismissing that which I don't. I'm fairly certain I couldn't have done the same at thirteen years old.

I hear a lot of young teenage boys talk about the 'sense of community' they find at the gym and that worries me. This 'community' of men are, in my experience, the ones who sit at the back, near the mirrors, with all the heavy lifting equipment. Every gym has them. This 'community' don't appear to have jobs because they are always at the gym, whatever time you go. Their lives pretty much revolve around muscle building. If we're not very careful, these men will become role models to young men who might not have many others in their lives (see 'role models' section in Chapter 4) and will become drawn into what can be a dangerous obsession, in addition to gaining disproportionate amounts of muscle their still-growing frames are not ready for.

Already, I am seeing how fitness and grooming regimes are undertaken by young men not in an attempt to attract a mate but to impress and pull rank on others within their peer group, a daft ritual traditionally associated with women.

Sam Thomas, founder of the charity 'Men Get Eating Disorders Too' expresses it better and more succinctly than I ever could when he says:

Masculine identity is ever-evolving, breaking down and becoming increasingly diverse in modern times. The result is that scores of men are 'lost' in terms of their personal identity, impacting on their self-esteem and confidence.

*Statistic from the Men Get Eating Disorders Too website

EXCERPT FROM 'NO WONDER YOUNG MEN HAVE A PROBLEM WITH SELF-ESTEEM'

By Natasha Devon

First published on the *Telegraph* website, June 2014

What can be done? Parents and teachers can create environments where young men feel safe and empowered enough to be vulnerable. Dads, uncles and male family friends can lead by example, instigating conversations around topics such as body image and mental health. The medical profession can supply the same level of understanding and resources for men suffering from issues such as eating disorders and depression as they do for women. Most importantly, as a society we can all work to reduce the stigma that still surrounds men who talk openly about their feelings.

We need to recognise that emotions have no gender.

HOW TO SPOT A BODY IMAGE ISSUE

One of the commonest questions I am asked by parents is how they should know if their child's body image habits are a cause for alarm. This is an eternal conundrum, because it's not as though we can opt out of eating or exercising or getting dressed. (Well, perhaps the last one. With mixed outcomes, I imagine.)

Unfortunately, the answer is that it's the motivation behind the behaviour, not the behaviour itself, or even the physical consequences (although they are a factor) which determines whether or not our habits are destructive.

Take for example the act of putting on makeup. Some people wear makeup because they are celebrating their face, enhancing features to draw attention to them because they like them. Some people wear makeup because they are apologising for their face, using cosmetics like a mask to hide behind because they are not confident enough to show their real face to the outside world. It's exactly the same action, with a different motivation.

Some people go to the gym because it's a convenient way to get their heart pumping a couple of times per week and we all know that's a good thing to do. Some people go because they are trying to mould the body they hate into a different shape. Again, same action, different motivation.

Some people avoid chocolate and crisps because they would rather eat food with more nutritional value and get maximum nourishment out of the things they consume. Others cut them out because they have a fear these foods will contaminate their 'clean' diet or are trying to severely restrict calories in order to bring about rapid weight loss. Same action, different motivation.

It's virtually impossible to merely look from the outside and determine whether or not the action has a healthy motivation. The only way to test the waters would be to gauge the reaction when routines are changed or metaphorical 'comfort blankets' are taken away. So, CAN the person in question leave the house without makeup on? If they cannot, this might indicate an issue.

Similarly, if the person becomes panicked at having to miss one gym session, or eating 'forbidden' foods, this may point to an obsession.

Of course there is the issue of quantity – frequency of exercise and how much/little a person is eating, but I'm always wary of using this as a hard-and-fast yardstick. With anorexia, for example, the illness should be characterised by how much the individual thinks about and controls their food intake, rather than how little they eat or how much they weigh.

Internal indicators are much harder to measure, but they are also much more reliable. In the early chapters of this book, Lynn speaks about using instinct to identify things like social isolation, which point to a wider problem. This might seem vague, but trying to measure body image issues using external markers often results in misdiagnosis, misunderstandings and delaying solutions.

Having said that, paying close attention to the language someone uses can give vital clues. In my experience, people with low body image self-esteem feel a relentless need to compare themselves to others. They'll often say things like '*Am I bigger or smaller than him/her?*' in reference to their friends, or people on television or in magazines. They feel a compulsion to know where their body sits in what they perceive to be a physicalised human hierarchy.

I'll never forget when a student of mine told me the story of the moment that made her see her body image issue clearly. She described herself as '*meandering into dangerous diet territory*' and was severely restricting her food intake. Her friends were having a sleepover and they were all sitting on the sofa in their onesies watching *X Factor*. Lady Gaga took to the stage to perform in her bra and pants and she asked her friends whether they thought she was bigger, or smaller, or about the same size as Gaga. At this point one of her friends turned to her and said:

'*For GOD'S SAKE, Sara! This is SO boring! I will literally talk to you about ANYTHING ELSE you want to talk about but I am NOT sitting here discussing whether or not your arse is bigger or smaller than Lady Gaga's! We are better than that!*'

In Sara's own words, '*That one sentence made me suddenly realise what a twat I was being. So I had some popcorn and talked about something else.*'

Which brings me nicely onto.....

USING LANGUAGE TO COMBAT BODY IMAGE WORRIES

There's so much focus on the visual when we discuss body image, we can sometimes forget how influential the language we use can be.

This is one of the few instances where, instinctually, we tend to do completely the wrong thing. Parents are always saying to me:

'*I tell him/her **all the time** he/she is gorgeous/perfect just the way he/she is.*'

And why wouldn't you? They have an issue with their body and you are reassuring them that their body is just fine as it is. It's completely logical to assume this would be the right approach.

However, we must always bear in mind that how we feel about our body is a reflection of what is going on in our mind.

How many times in your life have your heard someone use the phrase '*I feel really fat, today*'?

Just think about that for a moment. We're so used to hearing it we've lost sight of the fact that it makes absolutely no bloody sense as a statement, whatsoever. You can't 'feel' fat. Fat is not a feeling. It isn't like misery, or loneliness.

So what is that person actually saying to you? They're actually saying '*I feel fucking terrible about myself today but those feelings are too complex to unravel and express. Instead, I'm going to project them onto something tangible and easy to manage and talk to you about my body.*'

It's quite clear, then, that responding with '*Don't be silly, you are gorgeous just the way you are*' isn't going to address the root of the problem.

People with body image insecurities are in desperate need of reminding that their value lies in more than simply their exterior appearance. Again, this is more of a consistent, drip feed approach than something which can be achieved during a one-off conversation, but regularly reminding your students or children that you see, recognise and value qualities which cannot be captured in a selfie will probably slowly erode their body image concerns.

Girlguiding and Dove discovered that students whose school work was rated 'outstanding' were twice as likely to dismiss the prospect of having cosmetic surgery in the future as their classmates. This speaks volumes about the power of recognising talents you have outside of your physical appearance in building a foundation of body confidence.

We tell people they look lovely all the time. Yet we rarely take three seconds to acknowledge when someone does something kind, or thoughtful, or brave. From our earliest formative years, more of a fuss is made of us during occasions like weddings and birthday parties, when we are dressed in cute little outfits. The message children receive is '*The more effort I put into looking good, the more attention I will get.*'

Now, it would be utterly impossible to restrain ourselves from ever cooing over cute-looking small people. I know I'm not capable of it and I'm fairly certain no other human being is, either. Just the other day, I was staying in a hotel up North and saw two little girls dressed up for some sort of event in silk dresses with sticky-out skirts and big sashes around their gorgeous plump little bellies and I made that high-pitched sound that only women who have just seen something adorable can make. I also told them they looked beautiful. This is me we're talking about here, who has almost a decade of experience working in the field of body image and knows far, far better than to be that stupid.

So, working on the basis that banishing all talk of physical attractiveness is not going to happen any time soon, the only way to counteract the effect is to make an equally big palaver when children and young people achieve things other than looking nice.

As parents, the achievements you choose to emphasise are really at your discretion. Just work on the basis that whatever you praise your child for most often will come to be how they define themselves and therefore the quality they will most frequently exhibit throughout their lives. If I were you, I'd make a point of verbally rewarding kindness and bravery but that's just me.

A great tip I was given by a teacher once is to praise your children or students in a conversation with someone else that they can hear, but don't realise you know they are listening to.

That way the '*You have to say that you're my Dad/teacher*' argument is averted.

Similarly, I'm often asked by friends of teenagers who are self-harming or have an eating disorder what they can say to make things easier for their friend. This is a tricky one because, unlike any other mental illness, self-harm and eating disorders are, indisputably 'catching'. (This fact quite often doesn't go down well with the original person suffering, who will maintain that they are the ones with the 'real' problem and everyone else is 'copying'. Yet I've often been called into schools to deal with self-harm and anorexia 'epidemics' so that's just semantics, really. A problem is a problem, regardless of whether you thought of it yourself or copied it from somebody else.) Despite this, the worst thing we can do for the person experiencing the issue is isolate them so I'd never encourage their friends to withdraw contact in order to protect themselves.

Instead, I ask friends to practice the verbal habits above. Unless their friend sits down with them and says '*I am self-harming/bulimic and I'd really like to tell you all about it*' (in which case they should just listen and suggest they seek advice from a teacher or professional) friends should avoid addressing the problem directly. This is because a) they're not qualified counsellors and b) they run the risk of being sucked into the issue themselves.

There is a very wise thing my (equally wise) Mum always says on this particular topic:

If you were walking down the road and you saw a person in a hole, how would you help them? You might go and get someone else, or some rope to pull them out, or you might reassure them help was coming. The last thing you would do is get down in the hole with them. The only thing that would achieve is two of you in a hole, needing help.

Instead of figuratively climbing down into the hole, young people should find ways to remind their friend that they are appreciated for **who** they are, not **what** they are. They should take the time to say things like '*That was really funny*' if their friend makes them laugh. They should reminisce about happy times they had together. They can eschew the toxic nature of the issue whilst still playing a vital role in their recovery.

ADDRESSING BODY IMAGE ISSUES THROUGH ACTIVITY

I fully appreciate that this is not always the case, but body image played a gigantic, starring role in my own eating disorder. There are some people who have eating disorders who maintain the illness is either completely unrelated to body image or 'purely biological in nature'. Whilst I'd never tell them they were wrong, there is very little scientific evidence to back this up. I can't help but suspect these people fear that if body image is acknowledged as a component in their eating disorder, it will diminish the severity and status of their condition. There is a bit of denial going on, in my opinion.

At some point in my late teens, I embraced the notion that my only value to the world was in conforming to the prevailing beauty paradigm. It therefore did not matter what I had to sacrifice in order to be considered physically attractive. I constantly sought (and found) validation for how I looked but this merely fuelled the fire of my central and toxic belief.

Recovery was, for me, the process of rediscovering myself. I'd allowed my eating disorder to define who I was for so long, I'd become a stranger to myself. That involved working out what made me happy, what I was passionate about, what activities I enjoyed and what my opinions were. It was the process of re-engaging with the world.

I will never understand why in most instances the medical community's default response to diagnosed eating disorders is to lock patients away in a unit, together. Thus, we further isolate them from the outside world whilst actively encouraging them to pick up bad habits from one another. It's tough, particularly if someone appears too poorly and fragile to be let out into the big bad scary world, to encourage them to partake in activities, particularly if they're very physical. Yet it's absolutely necessary to allow someone to explore their environment if they are to escape the clutches of their illness.

Any body image issue can be tackled at least partially by giving someone the tools and the freedom they need to have the monumental realisation that there is more to life than their body. It might be through spending time with friends, sport, music, reading or arts – anything that reminds them who they are.

EXPRESSING INDIVIDUALITY TO TACKLE NEGATIVE BODY IMAGE

There are some people who will tell you that the definition of Body Confidence is rolling out of bed and immediately going out into the world completely 'au naturel'. Anything else, they will maintain, is an attempt to hide who we truly are.

This is, with the greatest respect, total tripe. Body confidence is being brave enough to show who you are using how you look, whilst accepting the things you cannot change. For some people that means eschewing cosmetics and grooming products. For others, it is painting a silver stripe down their face and dyeing their hair six different colours. In neither one of these examples is the person being any less 'themselves'.

I believe one of the things that makes the Self-Esteem Team popular is that we negotiate that precarious middle ground between not mindlessly marching along a path that will eventually make everyone look like Barbie and Ken, but not automatically condemning experimenting with or modifying the body, either. Young people have a finely tuned bullshit detector. Telling them that how they look doesn't matter at all was never going to be an effective approach. Instead we ask them to rock their 'own brand of gorgeous', making their outsides a reflection of who they are inside and to be proud of whatever aesthetic the mixture of their unique genetics and creativity creates.

In exactly the same way, I do not condemn beauty or fashion products. They can be a fantastic way to express yourself... IF you are expressing yourself, not the universal beauty paradigm.

For a lot of young people, particularly if they have a sibling or best friend who is considered to be very attractive, finding their own unique sense of style is incredibly helpful for their confidence.

I'm of the Gok Wan school of thought in this regard. I genuinely believe a great outfit can transform our attitude and outlook and I think everyone's style should reflect who they are. That's not the same as believing one's style **has** to be terribly *avant garde* or 'on trend'. One of the most genuinely confident people I know went to dinner at the Savoy in a thigh length grey cardigan without a scrap of makeup on her face. That was not only brave (because no one else there dresses like that) but a genuine expression of who she is which I can only applaud her for. She does not give one single fuck about style and just wants always to be comfy.

Your 'look' is exactly that. It's a way of telling the world who you are.

If all else fails, there is untold potential value in going shopping.

ADDRESSING AND EXPRESSING ADULT BODY IMAGE INSECURITY

Without doubt, one of the most effective ways to help young people combat their body image insecurity is for parents, carers and teachers to address their own. Children in particular are incredibly susceptible to throwaway comments, body language and overheard conversations, which adults might think nothing of.

Up to the age of seven we have no 'critical facility', meaning we cannot process and analyse the things which happen to us. We take them on at face value.

So let's say, for example, a mother tells her daughter that she is perfect and beautiful just as she is, but then goes on to criticise her own body within ear shot of her daughter. At very best, the message that the daughter receives is that body insecurity is part and parcel of being a grown up. At worst, she will take on the idea that a child's body is attractive but a woman's body is to be feared and rejected. This is likely to cause problems when the daughter hits puberty.

With boys, it's more a question of what the men in their lives **don't** say than what they do. If boys never hear their dads or male family members talking about body image, they will assume that they are the only ones who ever thought or worried about it. Adult men should lead by example, showing that it's okay to open up on body matters. In just the same way as with girls, this has to be approached correctly. Statements like '*When I was your age I used to be teased a lot for being short and it made me feel sad for a while, but now I realise it's a good thing and part of who I am*' can make all the difference.

CONCLUSION

During my life I have been fat, I have been skinny, I have been what society would deem ugly and I have been conventionally beautiful. Pre-recovery from my eating disorder, existing in each of these states was equally miserable. I never felt good enough and that feeling was not tempered or diminished by what the mirror, or other people told me about my appearance. One of the biggest lies we tell ourselves is that our lives would automatically be better if only we looked 'better'.

Body image concerns are almost always indicative of a wider issue. It may feel like you are going off-piste, but using techniques which recognise and embrace the whole self, rather than focusing just on the body, will often mean that body image worries dissipate as a consequence. Creating a high self-esteem environment at home and in school and leading by example as role models will also give young people a solid foundation, allowing them to find the requisite bravery to seek help for their own body issues.

Today, I am happy because I know that my body and the way I dress it, whilst part of who I am, are the icing on the cake. My value to myself and to the world lies in the sponge.

'YOU CAN BE TOO OBSESSED WITH HEALTHY EATING'

Natasha Devon

First published on the *Independent* website, February 2014

I began teaching body image lessons in schools in 2008. Back then, teenagers were pretty much exclusively concerned with the aesthetics of the body. Over the past few years, however, I've seen them become focussed, almost to the point of obsession, on the notion of 'health'.

This appears, on the face of it, to be progression… Except most young people's ideas about what constitutes health are not only woefully skewed, they're also being encouraged by certain sectors of the medical community, the media and industries intent on selling them potentially dangerous 'health' produce.

In my experience, most teenagers believe that health can be assessed by factors like weight and body shape. When I ask them how we know if we are healthy, they will invariably suggest hopping on the scales or looking in a mirror, rather than consulting our lifestyle choices.

Physical education teachers tell me it is now widely accepted for young men aged twelve and over to use protein shakes and lurid, liver destroying powders to 'help them perform' in competitive sports. 'Energy Drinks' – composed almost exclusively of sugar and caffeine – are marketed as a component of a 'healthy' regime. Boarding house mistresses confessed to me last week at a conference that their female pupils were ordering 'herbal' tablets designed to promote weight loss over the internet and when confronted were arguing that they were 'natural' and that the endeavour was being undertaken in the name of 'health'.

There appears to be no concept of moderation – going to the gym is considered 'healthy' no matter how obsessive or time-consuming the habit becomes. Eating any type of sugary or fatty food is universally dubbed 'unhealthy' no matter how much mental anguish and social exclusion the act of refusing that food might cause.

In school canteens, I now routinely hear teenagers claiming to be 'allergic' to wheat, dairy, gluten and sugar, or to be embarking on 'raw, vegan' diets they have seen espoused by celebrities in the pages of glossy magazines.

Well-meaning 'nutrition' lessons which are given to primary school children as young as five present health as a black and white issue, attaching moral judgements to basic biological functions – Fat = BAD, thin = GOOD. Biscuit = BAD, fruit = GOOD. Our children are being set-up for a lifetime of anxiety, food and body issues and, ironically, we're sowing the seeds of shame and guilt which form one of the primary factors behind binge-eating related obesity.

This week is Eating Disorders Awareness Week in the UK. 'Ortherexia' – a media-created term meaning 'obsession with health' is being labelled by some bloggers as the newest and most rapidly growing eating disorder trend, following the exposure it has received in the media. Susan Ringwood, Chief Executive of the charity B-eat, however, believes it is more complicated than that. She says:

> *The link to 'ultra-healthy' eating and exercise habits as a means of adopting a highly restrictive diet is part of a cultural context, as I see it. It used to be vegetarianism, then veganism, and now it's the issue of food purity. It's a growing part of the spectrum of eating disordered behaviour, because it's now culturally acceptable to say you are down the gym every night, or intolerant to wheat, or only eat raw food.*

So our culture of 'health' can be, in some respects, viewed as a new way to approaching an eating disorder. This is in the same week that we hear B-eat calling for changes to diagnostic criteria for more traditional eating disorders because these mental illnesses are STILL being measured by some GPs in stones and pounds. It appears that mental health, which is easily as important as physical wellbeing, is still consistently being pushed aside in the pursuit of a socially-acceptable body type.

The Health at Every Size (HAES) movement which has taken the US by storm is now taking root in the UK. Advocates (rather sensibly) claim that if we eat all food groups (paying special attention to consuming five fruits and vegetables a day), make sure we engage in regular physical activity (but not obsessively), drink enough water to stay hydrated, do not smoke and drink alcohol within the recommended guidelines then we are healthy, regardless of how we might look.

It isn't particularly groundbreaking or glamorous, but it

seems this old-fashioned advice of the sort your nan might have given you is the true path to physical wellbeing and is what young people need to hear.

CHAPTER 10

THE MEDIA

Natasha

Here is the basic structure of a conversation I have in various classrooms throughout Britain every single week:

Me: '*What do you think is the biggest influence on how we think we are supposed to look?*'

Class: *without hesitation* '*THE MEDIA!*'

Me: '*Okay, why is that?*'

Student: '*Well, they put all these images out there that are "perfect" and then that makes you feel like that is how you're supposed to look.*'

Me: '*Okay, why is that?*'

Student: '*Because they're all airbrushed and stuff and they use Photoshop so they're not even real but you still feel like that's how you're meant to be.*'

Me: '*And why do they do that? What's in it for them?*'

Student: '*Oh. Er.*'*shrugs* '*Not sure.*'

This is a clear indication of the way information about 'the media' is given to young people. We've deleted the most vital piece of information from the story, perhaps because we consider it to be obvious. This leaves young people believing media imagery is gratuitously cruel for cruelty's sake, a theory which dissolves under scrutiny, making as it does absolutely no sense whatsoever.

Young people are so used to hearing about 'the media' and how it's a terrible ogre of a thing hell-bent on destroying any shred of their dignity that blaming 'the media' for the way that they feel has become a default response. Of course, the day they spend time with someone who works in 'the media', or do some work experience in 'the media' and realise the ogre analogy wasn't entirely true, they'll assume they were lied to and abandon the entire train of thought. That's the trouble with sweeping generalisations.

There are a couple of really important things young people therefore need to understand about the media:

1. When people say 'the media' more often than not they are talking about advertising.

2. The media is usually responding to demand from the public, making it a reflection of our tastes.

ADVERTISING

It's easy to think 'the media' and advertising are the same thing, but they are not. Adverts permeate social media, television and magazines. They weave their way in, in the most insidious and surreptitious of styles and glare at us from virtually every screen, page or landscape. Lines have become further blurred because of the existence of something called 'advertorial copy' (which is an advertisement written as though it is an article) as well as widespread use of viral videos for marketing purposes.

The media relies upon advertising to survive. It doesn't matter how many copies of a newspaper or magazine are sold, it's pretty-much impossible to make a profit without hiring-out ad space.

Marketing can have a knock-on effect on media content. When I worked in the fashion industry, I watched the proverbial buck for routine use of size 0 models being endlessly passed from designers, to agencies, to magazines and even to the models themselves. Whilst it's true that most designers will refuse to supply magazines with anything above a size 6 or 8 (leaving them with no choice but to seek a model who fits into those clothes) this is arguably because they fear being ridiculed within an industry that still prises thinness above all other qualities, however much it might protest to the contrary. Publications that routinely use 'plus size' (i.e. size 10 and above) models also often find it difficult to attract and keep advertising revenue, without which they cannot circulate in meaningful quantities.

Television exists because huge amounts of money are paid to place ads within popular programmes. Social media is free for us to use because advertisers have bought space on websites and their money (as opposed to ours) pays staff wages. There can be absolutely no doubt that the media and advertising are inextricable, but they are not synonymous.

I have yet to meet a journalist, TV presenter or producer on my travels who has not sought to have a responsible attitude towards self-esteem, body image and mental health. I work closely with the teams at *Cosmopolitan* magazine, the *Telegraph* and *Independent* online, the *Sun*'s women's desk, ITV *This*

Morning and Sky News (a fairly broad remit) and can confirm everyone I have encountered has actively sought to empower their reader or viewer, albeit using different approaches. The media, as far as I can see, is choc-full of creative, sensitive people with good intentions. It is not in their interests for you, the viewer or reader, to come away from your experience of their product feeling worse about yourself.

Advertisers, conversely, depend upon you feeling apologetic about your body, lifestyle and home in order to thrive. To be completely fair to the industry, this isn't necessarily their fault. I'm sure there are creative, responsible, sensitive people who work in advertising, too, but the unpalatable reality is it's almost impossible to sell someone a product without convincing them that they need it. In order to convince a person they are in need of something, it is first necessary to highlight to them the ways in which they are currently lacking. This is fine when the underlying premise is '*I can't believe you're using that knackered old lawnmower*' but less fine when it's '*I can't believe you're walking around in that knackered old body.*'

Let's take the example of a skin product. Let's imagine I want to flog a foundation to the masses by way of a televised advertisement. I will probably use footage of a model who has spent five hours in makeup, been lit from every angle to make her appear 'flawless' and possibly even been photo-shopped frame by frame, if I can afford it. I will show the model turning her face this way and that, pouting seductively. Then a peppy, lilting voiceover will say: '*This foundation will even out your skin tone. It will conceal dark circles and blemishes, giving you an airbrushed look.*'

I'd probably follow up with a shot of my model donning a

leather jacket and hopping on the back of a waiting motorbike, being ridden by an impossibly handsome, well-dressed man before they zoom off into the sunset to do (it is implied) X-rated, sexy-type things.

As an advertiser, my job is done. I have visually and powerfully shown the (entirely unrealistic but not illegally so) effects of the product, whilst implying that it will make the consumer sexier, more popular and more beautiful. That is a standard way to market a beauty product and it has been shown to be effective in winning consumers for decades.

However, scant consideration (or perhaps just a complete disregard) has been given for the message which is taken on subconsciously by the viewer. For what my voiceover example has actually told them is:

You have uneven skin tone. You have dark circles under your eyes. For crying out loud, YOU HAVE SPOTS ON YOUR COMPLETELY UNACCEPTABLE FACE! My darling, you need to sort that shit out. I don't know how you have been walking around just, like, EXPOSING that face when clearly you need to look more like this airbrushed model.

The visual has then gone on to hammer that message home by unequivocally yet subtly stating that people who have blemish-free skin have better lives. The existences of the flawless-of-skin are exciting and glamorous... and what are you doing, viewer? You're watching this ad in your pyjamas, eating pre-baked cake mix straight out of the bowl, watching prime time, big budget karaoke on a Saturday night. The relative mundaneness of your life is because of your **stupid** skin, obviously! If only you had a better complexion, then you'd be flooded with social and sexual invitations, right now. THIS PRODUCT WILL TRANSFORM YOUR LIFE.

It would, of course, be utterly remiss to suggest that we are so gullible as to be won over by a single advert of this nature. I was fortunate enough to attend a lecture a couple of years ago by Dr Jean Kilbourne, who has devoted her professional life to studying the effect of advertising on our culture (and in particular the impact it has on our social perceptions of women). As Dr Kilbourne will tell you, the impact of advertising is cumulative. Together the billboards, bus stops, websites, television and magazine advertisements create an environment which is relentless in its message that we are not good enough, leaving us vulnerable and impressionable, i.e. the ideal consumer.

As a combined force, adverts create the impression of an imaginary party in the ether – one in which everyone is attractive in the most contrived possible way, wealthy, popular and they're all shagging each other. They invite you to buy their product as a token that will guarantee you entrance to this party. The trouble is, of course, the party does not exist. Your invitation will be lost in the post. Yet somehow we are still left feeling as though this is our fault for being fundamentally lacking.

If you think about it, the 'you can't join our party because there's something wrong with you' technique is one used by bullies throughout the globe. Advertisers might as well have provided a how-to guide in the art of bullying, demonstrating as they do the ability to say *'we are all over here enjoying ourselves without you and the reason you can't join us is because you are different - and that makes you wrong.'*

In essence, then, we are being bullied. We are being bullied in the street, in our homes and from our mobile phones thousands of times every week we are alive. And then we wonder at the burgeoning existence of the low self-esteem epidemic in recent years, when everybody began devoting significantly more time to the internet and watching television.

There are two reasons advertisers get away with bullying us in this way. The first is that they do it through visually pleasing imagery, with so much of their message being implied rather than explicitly stated. The second is that they get to us when we're not properly paying attention.

If we are on a social networking site, watching television, meandering down a busy street or flicking through a magazine, the chances are we are not intellectually switched on. Advertising is housed within vessels sought by people who have had a hard day and just want to relax and be entertained. We switch off our questioning facilities and let our brains have a rest. We make ourselves suggestible.

The solution, then, is to give young people the tools they need to question and dismiss false advertising ideals as a matter of habit, even when their brains have left the building. This can only be achieved through practice.

At home, I thoroughly recommend the act of sitting around the television as a family and shouting '*BOLLOCKS!*' at the screen when the adverts come on. It really is terrific fun.

At school, the art of questioning advertising culture can be practiced regularly in tutor time. The good thing about popular televised advertisements is a) they only last about thirty seconds and b) young people are always more than happy to watch them because they're colourful and shouty. Teachers can regularly pepper their tutor times with examples of advertising and ask students to distinguish between what the ad says and what it implies.

Students can be encouraged to read the small print, too. Small print demotes adverts from a terrifying power for potential self-esteem bashing evil to pant-wettingly hilarious. Legal disclaimers are flashed momentarily on screen, or listed in teensy weensy writing at the bottom of a page. They say things like:

Model is wearing hair extensions (in an advert for shampoo)

Model is wearing false eyelashes (in an advert for mascara)

Product will cause you to lose weight only if taken alongside a strict, calorie-controlled diet

Survey of 200 pre-existing product users (who, surprisingly, unanimously agreed that the product was fabulous).

My team and I have come under criticism before now for taking the approach that young people should adjust their world view to make them better equipped to deal with advertising onslaughts, rather than campaigning for advertisers to just STOPPIT.

Launching protests against specific advertisers is:

a. Not a particularly effective use of time and resources, since during the time it takes to protest against a specific advert, several more will be made in the same vein and several young people will be falling foul of their implied messages.

b. Counterproductive, since protesting efforts will probably garner headlines, thus securing publicity for the advert (in an age where all publicity is good publicity). A few thousand people will be moved to click on the online version of the advert, providing coveted click volume (the currency in which PR and marketing professionals deal) and making it seem as though whoever created the ad did a really good job. There's also a British mentality of 'don't tell me what to do' which will ensure a backlash which drives more people to view the ad and buy the product it sells out of sheer, petulant defiance.

The way I see it, giving children and young people the facility to apply a healthy dose of scepticism to the less palatable aspects of capitalism prepares them for whatever life might throw at them in that regard. Attempting to get one advert or image banned, conversely, metaphorically pisses in the wind.

OUR RELATIONSHIP WITH THE MEDIA

I wouldn't want you to think that, simply because I work within the media, I defend all of its actions unreservedly. You can be part of something and still deplore aspects of it you're not directly involved with. Just look at Charlie Brooker.

When I am Queen of Everything, all articles which centre around a 'weight loss journey' or which pretend to be about 'health' but are actually about a weight loss journey will be banned. If I never read a 'How I lost 7 stone in three seconds' style piece, about how the contributor used to be right proper miserable but now they can fit into a size ten they're SOOOOO much happier, it will be too soon. '*It's not about the weight, it's about the confidence*' they say, under an 800 word piece which documents exactly what they ate each day, how much exercise they did and what they weighed before and after with supporting pictorial evidence. (It makes my teeth itch that we live in a world where they couldn't just be happy whatever size they were and pledge to live a healthy lifestyle, with any resultant weight loss being an accidental bi-product and pretty much irrelevant.)

Since this is a book about self-esteem and mental health, I won't tell you how I'd also put the kibosh on articles which take an example of one family, who are in all reasonable probability representative of about one ten-thousandth of their demographic and happen to be fiddling their benefits, then use them as an example of how EVERYONE ON BENEFITS IS CHEATING THE SYSTEM. I will, however, direct you to the 'problem with modern awareness raising' section further along in this book for more relevant examples of, as the youth say, 'shit that needs to be squashed'.

The problem with the above examples, of course, is that they sell papers and they get online clicks, which is ultimately what the business of media is all about.

The people who balance the media's books don't care what motivates your click, or the sale of a publication, or the fact that you have watched a television programme. They do not care that you were left frothing at the mouth with indignation, or just watched out of morbid, car-crash style curiosity, or because you were bored. Viewing/readership figures are their cold, hard, completely emotion-free currency.

As I **keep** trying to explain to social media users who post links to articles and online videos which have outraged them, by imploring their followers to read/watch too because it's 'SO disgusting', all they are actually doing is ensuring that more articles are written in the same vein and similar videos continue to be made. It is the 'Nigel Farage blueprint for media interaction' (I just made that up. It's not a thing). It gives television personalities, journalists and the people who hire them permission to troll the nation by saying deliberately provocative, offensive and daft things in the pursuit of publicity.

One of my good friends is a showbiz editor. She is also an extremely talented writer and deeply empathetic human being, with a genuine desire to promote celebrities who are actively enhancing the world. I've lost count of the number of times she has lamented the fact that she wrote a fantastic article about, for example, Angelina Jolie's latest humanitarian venture and yet the clicks on it were outnumbered one hundred to one by people wanting to read about how a member of the cast of TOWIE who couldn't walk properly in their heels fell over in the snow.

So who should we blame when our sidebars are full of pictures of glamour models in bikinis 'enjoying a relaxing getaway' and the latest hedonistic exploits of Premier League footballers? Ourselves, that's who. We are the ones who demanded this tripe.

If young people want to see a better quality of media, they need to start watching, reading and sharing the good quality media that currently exists. This is the message I give to them, which I hope will be reinforced by teachers and parents:

Heard, seen or read something genuinely thought provoking and brilliant recently? Tell the world about it! Stop talking about the latest hokum being spouted by attention-seeking Z listers and the fact that you can see that singer's nipples through her dress. Realise that when you press a button which directs you to a video or article, or decide which channel you will watch, that is not a secret act you are undertaking in the privacy of your own home. That is information you are giving to the media about what is popular and what they should be doing more of. Do not allow curiosity to allow you to fuel the fire of something deliberately designed to be offensive. As young people, you are more powerful than you know. You dictate trends. So start dictating them on your terms.

Which brings me to.....

USING YOUR CONSUMER POWER

There are people doing wonderful things in the world of retail and marketing and if we want to see more from them (and less of the other) we have to reward them for their actions.

In the Google age, there is really no excuse for not knowing what policy your favourite brand of clothing or cosmetics has on body diversity, or animal testing, or using sweat shops. I ask my students to think of themselves as the poster boy or girl for whatever brands they use. In giving their money to these brands they are in effect sponsoring them to continue behaving however they are behaving currently.

If we do not like what we see, we can withdraw our cash and our attention. If we do like it, we can put our money where our mouths are. I'd caution at this point that we should always bear in mind the constraints put on retailers and media outlets by external forces they are powerless to control, some of which are mentioned above. Yet, despite this, there is undoubtedly a lot of progress being made in the world of fashion, beauty and fitness which deserves recognition and reward.

There are already far too many campaign Twitter accounts that relentlessly draw attention to things they deem to be morally offensive and invite social media users to retweet in order to demonstrate their outrage, as if that is going to solve the problem. It is as though they are in the business of telling young people how awful it is to be a young person, or women how terrible it is to have been born with the burden of being a female, when that energy could be much better expended empowering people by telling them all the reasons being young or being a woman is ace. Apart from anything else, being persistently encouraged to look at things which make you angry, or sad, or fill you with despair, is not terribly good for the mind-set.

Instead, the Self-Esteem Team share pictures, websites and blogs designed to uplift and inspire as well as links to retailers who are pioneers in the field of body confidence.

At the time of writing, for example, we are highlighting Debenhams for their use of a wide range of shapes, sizes, ages and races in their advertisements and online retailer ASOS for pledging not to Photoshop any of the models on their website. These are excellent practices which need to be rewarded, so we would encourage our online followers to spend their money 'sponsoring' these brands.

By regarding themselves as poster boys and girls for brands who are helping to make the world the kind of place they'd like to live, young people can influence their environment in a way that is not only tangible and pragmatic, but positive.

It also promotes what I like to call 'that feeling of YEAH!' There is nothing better than knowing you have put fire in a young person's belly, as well as giving them the knowledge that they are powerful and that their choices matter. It's another way for them to feel valued.

CHAPTER 11

HOW TO TALK ABOUT MENTAL HEALTH

Lynn

Mental illnesses tend to build up over time. They do not suddenly appear, like a broken leg, but progress and snowball. As soon as you feel that something is 'not quite right' it is important to trust and act on your instinct and try to address the problem. The longer mental health issues go on, the more ingrained they become and the harder they are to deal with.

The most effective way to intervene at this point is through communication. It's important to pick the right moment and location. It should be a time when it is just you and them, otherwise the young person might feel 'ganged up on'. It should also be in a place where they feel safe. Phones should be switched off so there is nothing to distract you.

Young people often worry that telling an adult will make things worse. You therefore need to be very clear from the beginning that you are there to support and help them and that you won't do anything without discussing it with them first.

Communication should take place in a straightforward manner. Don't assume that you know what the problem is. You might be mistaken and you run the risk of talking for ages about something that they can't relate to. Let them tell you about their feelings and fears first.

The most important thing is not to judge them, whatever they might confess to you. This will make them clam up. Show them that you respect their emotions and also their viewpoint, even if you disagree.

Watching for reactions is important. You can tell when you have hit on a sore point or are getting close to an uncomfortable subject by their eye contact, body language and how quick they are to defend themselves.

Remain calm. You are unlikely to feel calm inside but you must remain strong in the situation because if you are not the young person will start to panic. If you don't act as though there is a solution to their problem and everything will be okay then they may start to despair. They are looking to you as someone with the capacity to take their pain away.

What to Say

You might ask questions such as:

Can you tell me about what is happening?

How are you feeling?

I've noticed you are not quite yourself at the moment, is something wrong?

Have you ever felt like this before? When was that?

Do you feel as though you would rather talk to someone else about this?

What would you like to happen?

How can I help make you feel better?

Do you want my advice or would you rather I just listened? Acknowledge that the conversation is likely to be hard for them. Tell them that you are proud of the strength they are demonstrating in telling you about their problems. They might also be reassured if you tell them that there's nothing they could say that will make you stop loving them. Tell them it's okay to be frightened and they don't have to put on a brave face.

What NOT to Say

In order to write this section, I surveyed some people who had experienced mental health issues and asked them to tell me things their friends and family had said which they had found particularly unhelpful. All of these responses are completely understandable, but the tone is not right for the mind-set of a person battling a mental illness, and they are likely to make them feel misunderstood:

Why can't you just be happy?

Why do you always have to be like this?

Just pull yourself together!

Just snap out of it!

This is emotional blackmail.

How can you be so selfish?

Look at the effect this is having on the rest of the family!

This is all in your head!

I can't see why you can't just ignore this.

You're getting this out of proportion.

What do you have to worry/be depressed/be unhappy about?

Just think about something else.

Stop being so negative all the time.

Stop being so weird.

What's the worst that can happen?

All the above phrases create a barrier between the person experiencing mental illness and you, who are trying to help them. Getting cross and shouting will just make everyone feel worse. No matter how frustrated you might be feeling, it's important to put those feelings aside when you are talking to your child or student. Understand that feelings of depression, anxiety or self-hatred are all-consuming and cannot simply be pushed aside. Understand also that, as an adult, your library of coping mechanisms is much broader than theirs – you have dealt with numerous situations they have not. When you are experiencing anything for the first time it always feels more potent and urgent. It is crucial never to belittle their feelings, as they will seem overwhelming to them.

CONCLUSION

No matter how silly they might seem from the outside, mental health issues are very real to the person experiencing them. The kindest thing, I think, is to honour their reality and to work from within that in order to help them.

Everyone is different and mental health issues need to be approached on a person-by-person basis. People close to the sufferer can often try to 'talk them out of it', which is not always helpful but, as I have said, it is usually well-intended.

There's no definitive 'right' or 'wrong' way to do this, every family is different and (this is particularly true if you chose to seek outside help such as therapy) what works for one family might not work for another.

Open, non-judgemental communication should, however, always form the basis of your approach.

CHAPTER 12

MENTAL HEALTH AWARENESS RAISING – THE ISSUES

Natasha

When it comes to mental health conditions like depression, anxiety and bi-polar disorder there is undoubted value in simply making the public aware of the nature of the illnesses and dispelling the myths. However, from my earliest experiences of working with and speaking to teenagers, they made it clear that they felt that this kind of standard 'awareness-raising' lesson for mental health issues such as addiction, self-harm and eating disorders was both problematic and ineffective. They had all been in classes where they had been, essentially, schooled in the techniques they might use to damage themselves in some way. They had been given knowledge of the problems but no viable solutions.

This is a widespread problem and one I'd already experienced at first hand. When I first recovered from my eating disorder, like a lot of people who go through something similar, I was left thinking '*I really want to stop other people from doing that.*' As a consequence, I was plunged head-first into the incredibly toxic and confusing world of eating disorder awareness-raising and it taught me a lot about how I didn't want to be.

Online and in the press, past and present eating disorder sufferers wore their illnesses like badges of honour, competing to see who came closest to dying, who was hospitalised for the longest and who had the lowest weight. Not helped by the visual nature of most media, they posed in their underwear, citing weight loss and weight gain as indicators of success or failure, with no regard for whether or not they had healed the real problem, which is of course in their mind. Some of them had become 'cult leaders' online for other sufferers, gaining notoriety and adoration simply because they had been the 'most sick'. In some instances, it was clear that they were worshipped not for having conquered their illness, but simply for being able to reflect the thoughts and feelings associated with it on a relatively large platform. It was almost as though they were not concerned with helping others get better, but were attempting to convince the world that their eating disorder was justified, somehow morally righteous and made them special. They are essentially our modern day martyrs, cocooning current sufferers in a world where their illnesses make sense and there is no incentive to get better.

This is often how 'pro-anorexia' and 'pro-self-harm' websites emerge. They are created with a desire to build a community of people who understand and empathise with one another and become simply a forum in which users egg each other on toward more and more extreme behaviours. That's what makes pro-eating disorder sites so hard to identify, they are more often than not masquerading as support groups, run by people who have not conquered their own demons and are therefore in no position to provide guidance to others. This phenomenon is also partially responsible for the people who get locked into a state of being 'in recovery' from eating disorders for years and sometimes even decades of their life, having learned how to function on the most basic level and maintain an 'acceptable' weight, but not truly wishing to let go of an illness they have come to define themselves by.

This is more than a little fucked up, frankly. I can honestly say that during the time I had an eating disorder I never once did anything remotely 'special' in a positive way. I was too caught up in my illness to achieve anything, professionally or personally. It is, I believe, the fact of my recovery and what I have gone on to do since regaining my health that makes me a good role model for young people. When teaching my lessons, although referencing my own experience, I never mention any bulimia or anorexia 'methodology' and I never go into specifics about weight or food intake. Instead, I focus on what a momentous loss of potential my eating disorder was and how I got better. That is the salient information other people need to know.

About once a week, I'm emailed by someone who has had an eating disorder or self-harmed and '*really **really** wants to go into schools and tell children about what they went through.*' I can tell instantly from their tone that they are not someone I would wish to have on my team. Our lessons are not an opportunity to use a classroom of young people as makeshift therapists.

Nadia is the third member of my Self-Esteem Team and completes our trio perfectly by being the rock-chick muso-goth type to Grace's 'cool' and my 'glamorous' persona (when we go out together we are nearly always mistaken for a girl band). Nadia speaks to every young person who ever felt they weren't part of the 'in-crowd', having been bullied from a young age and finding her voice through a combination of journalism, rock music, dyeing her hair bright pink (years before Katy Perry did it, she wants you to know) and covering herself in tattoos.

Nadia struggled with self-harm from the age of ten. One of the first things we did in her training was find a way for her to talk about her own experiences without giving students tips on the various ways people self-harm, or either trivializing or glamorizing the issue. This is a very fine line to walk and can only be achieved if you take the attitude that sharing your story is merely a way of imparting information in an engaging way. As an educator, talking about past experiences shouldn't be cathartic for you: it should be useful to your audience. There is no room for ego. We had to find a way for Nadia to successfully convey the message: 'Self-harming doesn't make you weird or frightening, it comes from completely understandable, normal emotions – but it's not a healthy or desirable thing to do either.'

Having said that, talking about eating disorders, addiction and self-harm also necessitates being completely truthful about **all** the emotional aspects of the condition, even those which you fear will incur a negative judgment. Earlier this year, I was asked to review a book for the *Independent* called *How to Disappear Completely: On Modern Anorexia* by an author I hadn't yet heard of called Kelsey Osgood.

When the book arrived, I started gnashing my teeth in despair, assuming it would be yet another naval-gazing, 'awareness-raising' misery memoir, of which the bookshelves of the world are already woefully over-stuffed. I couldn't have been more wrong. By the time I reached the end of the book, Kelsey was one of my favourite people.

I so often read experts who say '*eating disorders are serious mental illnesses that have nothing to do with vanity or narcissism.*' I was beginning to think I was the only person in the world whose own experience of an eating disorder had a **lot** to do with narcissism and vanity, but feared publically expressing that sentiment in case I diminished the 'serious mental illness' part. When I was sick, I was attention-seeking and 'attention-seeking' has become synonymous with '*someone who should be ignored because they are being annoying and silly.*' Yet I was attention-seeking because I desperately needed (the right sort of) attention. Surely, we can acknowledge that most eating disorders are a form of attention-seeking whilst still recognising the seriousness of the conditions? So when Kelsey (very bravely) expressed almost identical sentiments, writing unpalatable home-truths about her own experience of anorexia with an almost-uncomfortable sense of clarity and self-awareness, obviously the only sensible response was for me to email her and tell her I loved her.

We've been pen-friends (or whatever the modern day email equivalent is) ever since and I think I may have found my American brain-doppelganger (everyone should have one).

In particular, Kelsey shares my passionate belief that we have as a society got our approach to eating disorder, addiction and self-harm education and awareness-raising completely wrong. In an age where everyone wants to be a celebrity, and we are giving a hefty chunk of attention and publicity to people with self-destructive illnesses, it must follow that some young people will emulate that behaviour simply out of a desire to get attention. 'Awareness raising' then becomes counter-productive, as it simply promotes damaging behaviours. She says:

What I've always felt to be the great catch to raising awareness about teenage mental health is the propensity such efforts have at actually providing self-destructive inspiration for young people.

Fact: teenagers are angst-ridden. Whether this emotional turbulence is rooted in their hormones, their genes, mounting pressure to conform to societal expectations, the increasing desire to assert their own identities even if through dangerous activities, or some combination of the above, its existence is indisputable. Exactly how and when self-destructive behaviour became popular amongst teenagers is a historical question, and one that I'm not qualified to answer, or to even speculate on. What we do know is that at some point, certain patterns began to emerge; recognizable trends in risk-taking began to emerge.

When people noticed these problems, they of course panicked, and thought, 'We need to tell all the kids not to do these things!' They handed teenagers pamphlets that listed alcoholic and anorexic behaviours, hand-outs with pictures of girls with heads bent towards empty plates of food, and posters with aphorisms blazing across a photograph of a scarred arm. And they thought: this is logical. That's where they were wrong. These 'awareness' campaigns can just alert the typical teenager to the many alternatives he or she has to express woe. In a byzantine way, the initiatives can inform the child what he or she should be doing: This is age-appropriate behaviour, and it is guaranteed to attract attention from your peers and, eventually, authority figures.

In today's culture, where so many fall foul of the consistent, myriad pressures we are under, we so rarely take the time to say *'well done'* to those who do manage to remain healthy and stable. Young people, who by their very nature want to be lavished with attention and praise, see recognition seemingly being given only to those who have issues in need of urgent attention. The squeaky wheel is getting the grease and for that reason some teenagers will inevitably make it their mission to render themselves squeaky.

Here is what **does** work:

• Conveying the absolute mental anguish and torture associated with self-harm and eating disorders, making it clear that eventually it will render one incapable of thinking about or doing anything else.

• Celebrating health and painting a vivid picture of how wonderful life can be once you have recovered from an eating disorder or self-harm.

• Emphasising that, whilst celebrities might speak publically about having gone through battles with eating disorders or self-harm, the moral to be taken from that is that no matter how rich, famous or talented a person is, they are still capable of suffering from cripplingly low self-esteem. (The message **not** to be gleaned is *'There is a fine line between genius and madness and destructive behaviours make me glamorous and interesting'*.)

- Discussing impact on social life and school work, rather than on physical health.

I remember once I was involved in a 'PSHE Day' where students are taken off timetable and go to a number of classes on rotation, one of which was an anti-smoking talk. At lunch, I was talking to a Year 10 girl who told me she smoked. I asked her how many cigarettes she smoked per day. Together, we worked out that if she gave up, at the end of the month she would be able to afford a skirt she really wanted from TopShop and at the end of the year she would be able to afford an iPad.

Just as I felt like I might be getting somewhere, the man who had been conducting the anti-smoking talks crept up behind us and bellowed, really loudly, whilst pointing at the girl:

'OH NO, YOU DON'T SMOKE, DO YOU? Think of what you're doing to your insides!'

You know when someone switches off and you actually see the shutters of their mind come down, so that you're not really looking at them anymore but the shell of a person who has completely disengaged? That happened. This young woman could not have made it more obvious that she had no more time for this conversation.

Teenagers in particular don't tend to care about the physical health implications of anything they do (unless of course they are trying to convince you of the virtues of their 'raw food fast' when it magically becomes paramount). This is partly because their brains are wired to take risks and push boundaries and partly because of the arrogance of youth – they simply assume they're going to live forever.

If we're going to discuss consequences, they have to be something immediate and relatable for it to be a deterrent.

Kelsey phrases it much better than I could:

You either think, with the bravado of youth, that you want to die or that you never will die, or some paradoxical combination of the two. When I was anorexic, I really believed that I wasn't afraid to die, but that was because I had no concept of death, or of things like osteoporosis, infertility, or cardiac abnormalities. What I find more compelling is to explain to teenagers that what might be considered acceptable or even cool as a teenager quickly becomes sad and lonely as you grow older. I tell them about how, right after I graduated from university at twenty-three, I started to notice my friends developing romantic lives, being engaged with their careers, planning their lives, and enjoying their surroundings, and I realised, like a brick to the face, that I wasn't going to have any of that.

Of course we must talk openly about mental health, but there is a duty to do so responsibly. It is important to reassure children and young people that feelings of anxiety and depression are normal and that if they are experiencing a mental health problem, they are not alone. Yet we must always take extreme care not to glamorise or normalise the physically destructive things we might do as a result of those feelings.

We must make young people feel special because of who they are and what they have vanquished in order to become who they are, not the simple fact of what they have been through. We must let them know that we believe them capable of conquering anything and, more importantly, that we will continue to be there for them when they do.

CHAPTER 13

SPORTS AND
THE ARTS

Lynn

In July 2014, a Primary School Head Teacher caused controversy by enclosing the following letter to her Year 6s, along with their exam results:

> *Please find enclosed your end of KS2 test results. We are very proud of you, as you demonstrated huge amounts of commitment and tried your very best during this tricky week.*
>
> *However, we are concerned that these tests do not always assess all of what it is that makes each of you special and unique. The people who create these tests and score them do not know each of you the way your teachers do, the way I hope to and certainly not the way your families do. They do not know that many of you speak two languages. They do not know that you can play a musical instrument*

or that you can dance or paint a picture. They do not know that your friends count on you to be there for them or that your laughter can brighten the dreariest day. They do not know that you write poetry or songs, play or participate in sports, wonder about the future, or that sometimes you take care of your little brother or sister after school. They do not know that you have travelled to a really neat place or that you know how to tell a great story, or that you really love spending time with special family members and friends. They do not know that you can be trustworthy, kind or thoughtful and that you try every day to be your very best...

The scores you get will tell you something, but they will not tell you everything. So enjoy your results and be very proud of these, but remember there are many ways of being smart.

Many journalists wrote scathingly about this letter, saying that it painted an unrealistic picture for children and that exam results and academic achievement are essential for getting a job. Those people missed the point entirely. Self-esteem is the key to engaging fully in anything in life, whether that be academic or social. Reminding children that they are unique and valued will help give them the self-esteem they need to tackle the challenges of life.

Furthermore, not everyone is academic and for those people school can be a very negative experience. Everyone is brilliant at something or passionate about something and it's important to discover what this is if we wish to have a strong sense of self.

Sport, music, arts and drama are essential parts of a rounded *education. They nurture children's creativity, giving them skills they can transfer to other lessons. They help to keep them healthy, both physically and emotionally and they also play a key role in building confidence.*

For those children and young people not fortunate enough to have a Head Teacher like the one who sent this letter, it's important that parents give them opportunities to experiment with sporting and creative activities. In any case, I would encourage parents to nurture their children's creative talents (although not in a pushy or aggressive way). Far from being 'extra-curricular' or 'things you do when you can't do anything else', these are skills that will help give young people mental equilibrium.

EXERCISE
Exercise is good for body, spirit and mind.

Activity and exercise are especially important for people living with mental illnesses, not least because people who have mental illnesses often have a higher risk of physical illness. Similarly, people with medical illnesses are at a higher risk of developing mental illnesses such as depression and anxiety. The body and mind exist in a balance, directly impacting one another.

By improving one's general physical health, the individual is at less risk of developing mental illness.

Scientists and research have shown that regular aerobic exercise can reduce anxiety and depression. They have discovered that exercise causes your brain to release chemicals that make you feel good, the same components which are included in anti-depressants

'Wouldn't it be great if exercise was prescribed as a first resort, rather than medication? With the correct support, motivation and education of exercise, an individual's awareness and image of themselves will improve. A healthy relationship with exercise can be a foundation for health and balance in other aspects of life.' *Ian Goodall, Fitness Coach*

Exercise can help to improve energy, concentration and sleep, all of which are essential to good mental health. Exercise can also help to focus the mind. When we exercise, especially if we are doing something we find challenging, it fills our head with the task at hand. So, for example, if we are running and getting tired, our entire attention is focussed on how hard it is to run, connecting us with our bodies in a primal way. Anything that might have been worrying us, stresses and anxieties, evaporate from the mind at this point because our brains don't have the capacity to think about them.

'Exercise has given me a stress release as it provides a change for my ever-active mind to stop focusing on the millions of things that are constantly in my head and instead concentrate all my energy, both physical and mental, into one thing.' *Lily, 16*

'Physical activity will help a person to feel good, releasing hormones that help them think positively. The benefits are both mental and physical. Working as part of a team to achieve something will develop an array of social skills that they can then transfer to everyday situations. Competing against others will also give them a challenge and focus that is needed in daily life.' *Leanne Poyner, P.E. Teacher*

Those who exercise regularly can have better body image and self-esteem. However, at this point I must emphasise that this is not always the case. In some instances, particularly in those relating to OCD and eating disorders, people with mental health issues actually use exercise to fuel their illness.

While exercise is an excellent preventative, someone with, for example, depression, may really struggle to exercise because they have fatigue or 'mental fog'. Although they may know intellectually that exercise will help, they may feel that they literally CANNOT walk round the block any more than they can fly to the moon. While gentle encouragement is likely to be helpful (as can praise if they do exercise) it's really important not to pressurise them into it, or you risk feeding into their feelings of unworthiness or hopelessness. They might think 'I'm so pathetic I can't even go for a walk.'

Exercise should never become an obsession. A way to tell if someone is exercising excessively is firstly by monitoring how often they exercise – it is recommended that young people take about half an hour to an hour's exercise per day. Unless they are training for something specific or part of a sports team it should not vastly exceed this. It's also important to monitor how the individual feels if their routine is changed. If they become anxious and panicked about missing one session of exercise then their habit may have developed into an obsession and intervention may be needed.

Exercise can also have a beneficial social component. Being part of a team or club can make young people feel that they have a sense of identity and belong to a loving network of people, united by their passion for a particular activity. Social skills such as losing and winning gracefully and working as a team can often be learned through interacting with others through sport. This is a much healthier way to socialise than via the internet!

'Being part of a boxing gym not only taught me the discipline I needed, it made me feel part of a family and gave me the guidance and confidence I needed to put my life back on track.' *Joe, 25*

One of the many people I met on my travels was Frank Bruno. His mental health issues have been well documented and at the time he was in the early stage of recovery from a bipolar episode in 2012. Frank has been very vocal on the importance of ongoing exercise as a contributor to the recovery period from a mental illness and he continues to use it as part of his daily life. I could only applaud his determination in this regard and encouraged him to carry on with his fitness regime.

'It was hard to exercise when on heavy medication. However even a small amount every day, building up the time gradually, for example starting by walking then running or going to the gym, is helpful. You don't have to be a body builder – look at it as part of your essential medication.' *Frank Bruno*

DRAMA

I have seen first-hand how participating in drama has enhanced the sense of self and mental wellbeing of my own daughter. Samantha began doing drama workshops at a local theatre when she was well into the recovery process, but still felt there was 'something missing'. Being a naturally shy person, drama gave Sam the safe space she needed to explore emotions. It has completely transformed the way she sees herself and given her the confidence she so desperately needed. In some ways I would say that it is drama that completed her recovery from her mental illness.

Drama has a number of benefits for people with low self-esteem. In drama we learn how to inhabit another character. If young people can then channel this skill and use it to create a confident version of themselves, they can practice walking, talking and behaving in positive ways until these habits become second nature.

'Drama can help with mental illness by themes of inclusion, memory and escapism, by taking on another character. Self-esteem can be promoted by being part of a team, relying on others, progression, and reward from rehearsals to the finished show.' *Charlie Brooks, Actress and Drama Teacher.*

Teenagers are not very empathetic by their nature. Neuroscientists have shown that the ability to empathise with others is a skill we actually develop fully around about the age of twenty-one. This can negatively affect self-esteem. If we do not understand what motivates other people to behave the way that they do, we can end up believing that everything that happens around us is a reflection on us. People with low self-esteem often feel guilty for no reason at all. Drama helps them to think about why characters might act the way that they do and understand that human beings are complex and not everything centres around them.

For shy young people, drama is one of the few times in their lives where they can step out of the label of being a shy person. They are given permission to scream and shout and laugh without judgement. Drama pushes young people's boundaries, helping them to realise that they don't have to always conform to the label they have been given. It can allow them to realise what they are capable of.

'Over the last two years my love of drama and music has taken me to the end of my comfort zone and beyond. It has pushed me to limits I never thought I was capable of.' *Samantha, 23.*

Most plays and TV shows are about consequences too. Looking at a human story from the outside, young people can identify the ways that the characters might have made different decisions to bring about a more positive outcome. They can then apply this to their own lives, realising that they do have the power to influence what happens around them.

'Young people need an outlet to explore human possibility. It is vital that they understand the power and potential of their own voice to affect change and we must provide them with a framework to do so. Unprecedented levels of

pressure to compete and succeed, in addition to the endless airbrushed images in the media, mean it has never been more important for young people to walk tall and love themselves, because of their flaws, not in spite of them.'
Ciaran McConville, Director of Learning & Participation, Rose Theatre Kingston

---

MUSIC & ART

Some young people find it really difficult to express how they are feeling with words. They might even feel that what they are going through CAN'T ever be expressed adequately by words alone. For these people, a creative outlet might help them to explore and exorcise negative feelings and embrace new and positive ones.

Art and music therapy has long been shown to increase the effectiveness when used alongside traditional therapy methods like counselling and CBT. These activities often have a cathartic quality in themselves, without needing to be analysed.

'I have realised that the only way to get my emotions out in a healthy way is art. Now literally everything I feel comes out in my art. Usually I don't realise until I've finished and suddenly feel better. I look back at my work and see something very familiar!' *Charlotte, 22*

In just the same way as drama, art and music are reflections of the human condition. They allow us to explore how we feel and behave and why, in a safe and healthy way. They can also evoke emotions. Young people are often frightened of expressing feelings like sadness and so keep them cooped up. Music and art can connect them to their inner voice. They can be a way of unravelling complex or frightening situations and emotions.

'Music can evoke strong feelings and memories. This process can with the latest psychological techniques be nurtured and created deliberately. This process could be used to create strong associations between self-esteem and a well loved music track.' *Neil Long, Radio Presenter, Voice and Confidence Coach*

If a young person is particularly 'into' an artist or band, this also helps them form a sense of identity and connect with others who think in similar ways, decreasing any sense of isolation.

CONCLUSION

Exercise, drama and the arts are ways of making young people realise that they are more than their exam results. Even if they are high academic achievers, the subsequent pressure as they define themselves as 'the one who is always the best at everything' can be huge. These less academic activities are an essential part of life, allowing us to explore our relationship not only with ourselves but with the world and to develop key life skills.

They can also be a powerful tool, not only in tackling mental health problems, but in maintaining good mental health at the end of the recovery process.

CONCLUSION

Lynn

When I set about writing this book, my primary aim was that above all else I should not patronise our readers, or give the impression that I have the 'perfect' family (or even that such a thing exists!). I hope I have achieved that.

I know exactly how hard it is to deal with mental health issues in the home. I have walked that walk. What I learned is that promoting good mental health and high self-esteem is all about the small, simple things we do on a daily basis, which are so much more valuable than big, dramatic gestures.

There is no more valuable commodity than time and yet this is the thing we are most short of in the modern world. As parents, we can only make time for our children, listen without judgement and act on our instincts.

Mental ill-health cannot be seen and yet has the potential to do just as much damage as physical ill-health. Great progress is being made by organisations like Young Minds to decrease stigma and provide help and support. Attitudes are changing – slowly. I hope that we will come to place as much importance on giving our children self-esteem as we do giving them hot meals and clothes on their backs. It is just as important for them to have the protection they need to be able to go out into world and fend for themselves.

Habits are powerful things. Bad habits can create huge problems and good habits have the potential to solve them. This book has really been about tiny changes that lead to good habits within the home and at school. Just by asking the right questions you can give your child the message that you are open to communication and that they are unconditionally loved.

You can lead by example. Raising a child is a team effort, involving parents, carers, extended family, teachers, friends and GPs. We all need to be working towards the same goal.

Let's start a good habit revolution and give generations to come the most crucial of all life skills: Resilience.

I'd like to give my last word on this to my godson, Ed:

A healthy lifestyle isn't just about eating right and exercising. Having good people around you can help to support you mentally and will normally be the people to pick you up when you are down.

Natasha

Many of the social factors which contribute to poor mental health and low self-esteem are so deeply entrenched in our culture, I cannot imagine a time when they will ever be fully extracted. I hope I am wrong. In the meantime, the only thing we can do is give young people the armour they need to successfully navigate the society we have created for them.

I believe one of the most effective ways we can do this is to re-examine increasingly linear attitudes towards education. With each year that passes, I see the right-wing press whipping themselves up into more of a state of indignant fury at what they perceive to be a lack of intelligence, skill and employability in today's young people. Under the Tory/ Lib Dem coalition, I've seen a streamlining of the curriculum to give precedence to traditionally 'academic' subjects. At the same time, I've heard and seen things which reveal a latent social mistrust of teachers.

I wish more than anything that everyone could understand what I understand, having worked in more than 200 UK schools. Young people are far from lazy and stupid and if they are being failed it is almost certainly not their teachers who are failing them, but the system. We have failed to grasp that children were much happier, healthier and performed better academically when they weren't rigorously tested from the age of four, when they weren't victims of a target-based education system and when 'non-academic' subjects like sport, music and PSHE where given more priority within the curriculum.

For those concerned only with exam results, it is necessary to understand that academic achievement and good mental and physical health go hand in hand. We cannot neglect a young person's wellbeing and expect them to perform to the best of their ability. For the rest of us, including the countless teachers I have spoken to on the subject, we need to hammer home the message that a school education is about more than getting a job at the end of it. In the words of a wise Head Teacher I heard speak at a Parliamentary meeting: '*We need to start thinking about the sort of citizens we want to be turning out at the end of the schooling process.*'

I never cease to be amazed by how much teachers' time is taken up dealing with pastoral issues. I know the strain this must place on an already overstuffed schedule. That's why there is a need for people like my team and Kelly Young and Rachel Beddoe and all the other wonderful people who come from outside agencies to work in tandem with teachers and parents to tackle these issues. But schools need funding to invite us in. They also need up-to-date guidelines from experts on subjects like sex education and sufficient space within the curriculum to create more of a balance between academic and emotional education.

That's why, in September 2013, I wrote an open letter to the Secretary of State for Education (then Michael Gove), asking that the government step in to help the huge swathes of young people struggling with mental and physical health issues and the teachers supporting them. The letter was first published on the *Telegraph* website and in the *Huffington Post*. We later published it on the website of body image charity Body Gossip, where you can still find it today and sign it to indicate that you agree with its contents. I have reproduced the original letter below.

When this book is published, I plan to take a group of my former students to Parliament to explain to the current Education Secretary why top-quality PSHE in schools is so crucial. At the time of writing, the Secretary of State has declined my (numerous) invitations to set up a meeting, in language that suggests the department assumed it's for some sort of A Level project and not terribly worthy of their time or energy. I will not stop trying and the more signatures I have, the more convincing a case I can build. I hope you will lend your support.

AN OPEN LETTER TO THE SECRETARY OF STATE FOR EDUCATION.

I am Director of the Self-Esteem Team, which provides what is currently the UK's most in-demand self-esteem and body image education programme in schools and colleges throughout the country.

In a world where one in ten young people will develop an eating disorder before they reach the age of twenty-five (with 1.6 million currently officially diagnosed and millions more hiding their symptoms and suffering in silence); where in a typical British classroom three children are currently self-harming; where online bullying has led to three high-profile teenage suicides since the beginning of 2013; where 30 per cent of boys and 70 per cent of girls aged eleven to nineteen cite their relationship with their body their 'number one worry' and emotionally-motivated obesity is spiralling, the wonderful teachers we have worked with have shrewdly identified the need for a class like ours.

We have worked with more than 40,000 UK teenagers to date, male and female, in State and Independent education. We use a combination of first-hand testimonial, psychology and media literacy to make our students realise they are both valuable and valued. We give them the tools they need to navigate the worlds of internet, media, fashion, beauty, food and exercise and are the catalyst which often allows them to become healthy, happy and to fulfil their potential. We're helping young people approach their education, social life and future with confidence and we're doing it with the one hour of a student's entire education schools can spare from their academic timetables.

In September 2013, a spokesperson from your department spoke of classes containing *'bogus pop psychology based on self-image'* which are *'no substitute for the real facts of education'*. This suggests your team believe that our agenda is at odds with your own, which you have always maintained is to raise academic standards in this country. To achieve your goals, you as Secretary for Education have deemed it necessary to place more emphasis on core, traditional academic subjects, remove the budget for Personal, Health and Social Education in state schools, refuse to raise the amount of time spent in physical education to a minimum of two hours per week and cut huge swathes of vocational qualifications from the curriculum.

Whilst I cannot condone the way in which your policies have in my opinion ostracised those young people whose talents fall outside the traditionally academic, I am actually writing to outline how our classes and other expertly delivered PSHE can and are assisting you in your agenda. I agree entirely that British children deserve the best possible education and should be encouraged towards the highest academic standards they are capable of. However, academic and emotional education are not mutually exclusive and they are not opposed to one another. They must, crucially, work in tandem if young people are to truly benefit from an excellent school experience.

The best Maths and English in the world won't help a student pass their exams if they are occupied by –

Being pregnant at fifteen

Being sexually confused

Having an STI

Taking drugs or binge drinking

Have an eating disorder

Self-harming

Having a pornography addiction

Being bullied, either in person or via the internet

Suffering from depression

Having a mental illness and being misunderstood

Or if they are simply crippled by self-loathing

You have often spoken about the need for the issues listed above to be addressed at home. The fact is, we cannot control what happens between the closed doors of every British household, but you are in the privileged position of having influence over what happens in every British school.

The world is not as it was when you (or even I) were at school. It has never been more difficult, more fraught, pressured and frightening to be a teenager. At school, young people are developing health issues – both mental and physical – which go on to cost the NHS billions of pounds every year. They need our intervention and they need our help – help delivered by the very best experts in the field, not in-house teachers who are already stretched to capacity. For this to happen schools need a budget – an investment from you which will be paid back to the taxpayer a hundred times over in the future.

Over 60 per cent of our business presently comes from Independent schools, despite 93 per cent of British children being educated in state schools. You have recognised Independent schools as producing the highest exam grades. Could this be because they also have the money at their disposal to run the most robust, thorough and imaginative PSHE programmes?

Could the fact that they also tend to devote a lot of time and money to sports and arts programmes for their students also play a part?

I am writing to you to beg you not to let the partisan rhetoric that has blighted Tory politics of late filter down to the sphere of young people's education. Please stop presenting the situation as a battle between those committed to academic excellence and those with a desire to incorporate lessons relating to the realities of modern life. There is no battle. The future of our young people is too important to create bogus divisions within the education sector for your own political gain.

Yours sincerely

Natasha Devon

To sign the petition, go to www.bodygossip.org/petition

Please note that, throughout this book, some names have been changed to protect identity.

ACKNOWLEDGEMENTS

Natasha

Thank you to my 'sounding boards' – my Mum (Christine) and my partner (Marcus) – for all the times you've heard me say *'Can I just run this by you to check it makes sense...?'* and didn't respond with *'No actually I'm not in the mood/want to watch Eastenders/am desperate for a wee.'*

Thank you also to my Dad (Paul) for giving advice throughout my career which has ensured my musings on self-esteem have never entered the realms of 'fluffy marketing bollocks'; to Uncle Andy and 1C2R Elizabeth for imparting countless pearls of wisdom from your many combined years working in education; and to the 'Self-Esteem Team', Grace and Nadia, not only for your dedication to spreading the word but for all the occasions when I've slumped on a pub table screeching *'I CAN'T DO IT ANY MORE I'M TOO TIRED'* and you have ever-so patiently explained why I was being a daft tit.

Finally, thanks to Lynn for co-authoring, but more importantly for all the pitta bread and hummus.

Lynn

Thank you to my wonderful husband Kevin and our beautiful daughters Charlotte and Samantha, our unconditional love for each other has enabled us to face life's challenges together, always emerging stronger and more united for it.

Warm thanks go to my fantastic loyal friends Kate, Wendy, Jill, Gerry, Kyra, Shauna, Leanne and Andyj.

Thank you to all my clients both past and present for trusting me enough to share their journeys with them.

Special thanks to John Dalzell, Dave Spinx, Dionne Curtis, Jamie Baker, Michelle Morrice, Charlie Brooks, Carina Skinner, Neil Long and Barney Ferris for helping to fit the final piece in Sam's puzzle.

My wonderful Mum, you have been my strength over the past two years, never judging, just supporting and always with unconditional love and a big smile – thank you.

Last but by no means least my co-writer Natasha Devon and all at John Blake Publishing who have made this book possible.

FURTHER SOURCES OF HELP & INFORMATION

To find out more about Lynn Crilly go to www.lynncrilly.co.uk
To find out more about Natasha's self-esteem classes go to www.selfesteemteam.org

FURTHER INFORMATION/CONTACT FOR CONTRIBUTORS

Young Minds
YoungMinds is the UK's leading charity committed to improving the emotional wellbeing and mental health of children and young people.
Website: http://www.youngminds.org.uk/

Kelly Young
Kelly delivers school workshops addressing online pornography and works in Cardiff and the neighbouring counties.
Contact: Kelly.Young82@hotmail.com

Grace Barrett

Grace is a singer/songwriter and member of the Self-Esteem Team, delivering workshops all over the UK.

Website: www.mykinkyafro.com

London Faerie

Faerie provides workshops and counselling for people keen to explore their sexuality and the implications for other areas of the lives.

Website: www.londonfaerie.co.uk

Jake Basford

Jake is a contributing writer for a number of LGBT publications, as well as an ambassador for the charity Body Gossip (see below).

Contact: www.twitter.com/MooseyJake

Ian Goodall

Fitness Coach

Website: Twentyfitness.co.uk

Frank Bruno MBE

Frank Bruno is available for personal appearances and speaking whether motivational, mental health orientated entertainment, boxing or other subjects. His memorabilia is used by charities and fund raisers all over the world.

Website: www.frankbruno.co.uk

Contact: info@frankbruno.co.uk

Neil Long

Neil is a radio presenter, voice and confidence coach
Facebook Page: www.facebook.com/neillong1078

Mark Jermin Stage School

'*A school where pupils are valued, where real confidence is born and harnessed, and where ambitions are recognised, encouraged and achieved.*'
Tel: 01792 45 88 55
Email: info@markjermin.co.uk
Website: www.markjermin.co.uk

The Rose Theatre, Kingston

Website: www.rosetheatrekingston.org/takepart

For a comprehensive range of mental health techniques, tools and tips visit www.withhopeonline.com.

RECOMMENDED FURTHER READING

Teenagers: A Natural History by David Bainbridge (Portobello Books Ltd, 2010)
Surviving Girlhood: Building Positive Relationships, Attitudes and Self-Esteem to Prevent Teenage Girl Bullying by Rachel Beddoe and Nikki Giant (Jessica Kingsley Pub, 2012)
Hope with Eating Disorders by Lynn Crilly (Hayhouse Insights, 2012)
Body Gossip: Celebrities and the Public Unite to bring you the Real Story of the Great British Body' by Ruth Rogers and Natasha Devon (Rickshaw Publishing, 2012)
'*How to Disappear Completely: On Modern Anorexia*' by

Kelsey Osgood (Overlook Press, 2013)
How to Leave Twitter: My Time as Queen of the Universe and Why This Must Stop by Grace Dent (Faber &Faber, 2011)

RECOMMENDED FURTHER SOURCES OF INFORMATION AND SUPPORT

Head Meds – Information for young people on mental health medication – www.headmeds.org.uk

Rethink Mental Illness – Challenging attitudes around mental health – www.rethink.org

A range of mental health tools, techniques and tips (developed by Lynn Crilly & others) – www.withhopeonline.com

B-eat – National charity supporting people affected by eating disorders – www.b-eat.co.uk

Men Get Eating Disorders Too – support for men with eating disorders – www.mengetedstoo.co.uk

The Cybersmile Foundation – tackling all forms of online bullying/hate campaigns – www.cybersmile.org

National Self-Harm Network – support & advice for those affected by self-harm – www.nshn.co.uk

OCD UK – working with children and adults affected by OCD – www.ocduk.org

Beat Bullying – international bullying prevention charity – www.beatbullying.org

Body Gossip – A charity promoting body confidence – www.bodygossip.org

Make Love Not Porn – realistic sex information and videos for young people - www.makelovenorporn.com

Scouting for Jobs – websites to help former Scouts and Guides find employment – www.scouting4Jobs.com and www.

guidingU2Jobs.com

All Walks Beyond the Catwalk – A campaign to bring more diversity into fashion advertising – www.allwalks.org

'Killing us Softly' – Short documentaries on the effects of advertising by Dr Jean Kilbourne (search www.youtube.com)